ANTHEM

Ayn Rand

AUTHORED by Bella Wang
UPDATED AND REVISED by Damien Chazelle

COVER DESIGN by Table XI Partners LLC
COVER PHOTO by Olivia Verma and © 2005 GradeSaver, LLC

BOOK DESIGN by Table XI Partners LLC

Published by GradeSaver LLC, www.gradesaver.com

First published in the United States of America by GradeSaver LLC. 2009

GRADESAVER, the GradeSaver logo and the phrase "Getting you the grade since 1999" are registered trademarks of GradeSaver, LLC

ISBN 978-1-60259-188-2

Printed in the United States of America

For other products and additional information please visit
http://www.gradesaver.com

Table of Contents

Biography of Rand, Ayn (1905-1982)...1

About Anthem...5

Character List..7

Major Themes..9

Glossary of Terms...15

Short Summary...17

Quotes and Analysis..19

Summary and Analysis of Chapter One..25

Summary and Analysis of Chapter Two..29

Summary and Analysis of Chapter Three..33

Summary and Analysis of Chapter Four..35

Summary and Analysis of Chapter Five...37

Summary and Analysis of Chapter Six..39

Summary and Analysis of Chapter Seven..43

Summary and Analysis of Chapter Eight...47

Summary and Analysis of Chapter Nine..49

Summary and Analysis of Chapter Ten..53

Summary and Analysis of Chapter Eleven...57

Summary and Analysis of Chapter Twelve..61

Suggested Essay Questions..65

The Case Against Objectivism...69

Table of Contents

Author of ClassicNote and Sources..71

Quiz 1..73

Quiz 1 Answer Key..79

Quiz 2..81

Quiz 2 Answer Key..87

Quiz 3..89

Quiz 3 Answer Key..95

Quiz 4..97

Quiz 4 Answer Key..103

Biography of Rand, Ayn (1905-1982)

Ayn Rand was born on February 2, 1905, in St. Petersburg, Russia, as Alissa Rosenbaum. During her younger years she lived a comfortable, affluent, middle-class existence. Her father Fronz had become a chemist despite quotas on Jews studying at the university. Her mother Anna subscribed her to children's literary magazines, which inspired her to write her own stories. (According to the Rand mythology, she decided to become a writer at age nine.) In 1917 she and her family witnessed the Russian Revolution as the Communist party took over the government. The family lived in relative poverty from that point on, for her father did not have many friends in the new government.

At age 16 in 1921, she enrolled at Petrograd State University. During her second year she was expelled as anti-proletariat, but thanks to protests by foreign governments, she was reinstated. After she finished her degree, she enrolled at the State Technicum for Screen Arts, where she studied screenwriting. At this point Rosenbaum (Rand) knew that her philosophy did not fit with the Communist agenda, and realized she needed to leave Russia. In January 1926, she got a passport to visit relatives for a short time in Chicago, but she never returned.

As a child, Rand had been particularly influenced by Maurice Champagne, Victor Hugo, and Friedrich Nietzsche. Respectively, these authors gave her intelligent, independent protagonists as role models, showed her the power of a complex story with larger-than life characters, and taught her about the importance of heroism and individualism, although she did not necessarily agree on all points with the authors. In addition, Rand's negative experiences with communism caused her to become a lifelong opponent of Communism, although she remained an atheist in the manner of Nietzsche (Concise Dictionary of American Literary Biography Supplement: Modern Writers, 1900-1998).

Soon after her arrival in Chicago, Rand left for Hollywood, hoping to get a job as a screenwriter. Around this time she changed her name. In addition to the usual reasons that people change their names upon entering Hollywood, Rand may have intended to protect her relatives in Russia, who could be punished for the ideas and arguments she was planning to express through film.

Rand claimed that she arrived in Hollywood with only fifty dollars in her pocket and that the day after she arrived in Hollywood, she was given a car ride and a job as a movie extra by film director Cecil B. DeMille. While this account is probably at least partially untrue, Rand did work as an extra in several of DeMille's films. In fact, it was on the set of DeMille's film *King of Kings* that she met her future husband, actor Frank O'Connor.

Rand's career as a writer was launched in 1932, when she successfully sold a screenplay to Universal Studios. While the film was never produced, she then wrote the play *The Night of January 16th*, which was produced on Broadway in 1934. Her first novel, *We The Living* (1936), portrays life in post-communist Russia. In the preface Rand readily points out the autobiographical similarities between her own youth and the life of her protagonist. However, it was negatively reviewed in a time when many educated thinkers were in favor of the ideal of Communism. This novel was followed by *Anthem* (1938), a science fiction novel about a future dystopia where the world has been corrupted by communism. Rand did not enjoy real success until the publication of *The Fountainhead* in 1943. Rand's last novel, which most consider her masterpiece, *Atlas Shrugged*, was published in 1957.

Rand introduced what she called Objectivism through a 60-page speech given by the hero, John Galt, in *Atlas Shrugged*. In *Atlas Shrugged*, Rand characterizes Objectivism as "the concept of man as a heroic being, with his own happiness as the moral purpose of his life, with productive achievement as his noblest activity, and reason as his only absolute." She also states in her writings that Objectivism is intended to be a practical philosophy grounded in man's ability to reason. In a speech in 1963, Rand summed up her views. "The motive and purpose of my writing is the projection of an ideal man. The portrayal of a moral ideal, as my ultimate literary goal, as an end in itself – to which any didactic, intellectual or philosophical values contained in a novel are only the means." John Lewis writes of her, "Her vision of the ideal man was a theme uniting her early life, her literary career and her later philosophical work." (Literary Encyclopedia).

Rand also proposed a theory of aesthetics which she publicized in a series of essays published between 1965 and 1971. According to Louis Torres and Michelle Kamhi, "Rand's esthetic theory forms an integral part of her total philosophic system . . . *Objectivism* [is] a neo-Aristotelian philosophy of individualism based on reason and an objective view of reality" (15). Rand usually named Aristotle as her most important philosophical influence, though Nietzsche also had a clear influence on her. She also claimed to have been inspired by John Locke's ideas about property.

One of the fundamental problems of learning about Objectivism is that almost no one has written about it who is not a proponent of it. Those who disagree with Objectivism tend to argue that Rand's philosophy is not important enough to write about (for instance, that it is a weak derivation from Aristotle with some other ideas thrown in), so there is minimal significant literature critiquing it. Rand is also controversial as a literary author because of the intense academic disagreement about whether her books should be studied as literature or whether they are merely popular novels. One should note that Rand intended to remain outside of academia because of her many criticisms of it, and she did not see the need to be accepted by the academy. Perhaps she was afraid she would not be taken seriously as a philosopher without a Ph.D. or other relevant formal training. Moreover, the very argument for Rand's *popular* importance, her popularity in some quarters, is explicitly rejected in *The Fountainhead*. Another possible explanation of Rand's unpopularity in academia is that in 1947 she testified before the House Committee on Un-American Activities about communist penetration of the film industry. Although many now do not know of her choice in this case, at the time it would have been likely that Rand would be called a fear-monger and a traitor to certain American ideals in that she chose not to defend a person's right to be a member of the Communist Party.

Another event that may have influenced Rand negatively is a scandal that surrounded her and her coterie (known as the Collective). In 1949 Rand began corresponding with a young man named Nathan Blumenthal. By the late 1950s, Nathan Blumenthal (who had changed his name to Nathaniel Branden) and his then-wife Barbara were at the center of a group of young intellectuals who were devoted to Ayn Rand--both to her works and to Rand personally. Branden formed an institute with the intent of sponsoring lectures and publications on her philosophy. At some point during this time, Branden stated, their relationship moved beyond friendship. For almost a decade Branden was Rand's biggest supporter, advocate, and colleague. In 1962 he and Rand started the *Objectivist Newsletter*, which became a small magazine called *The Objectivist* by 1965. According to Branden (his claims are supported by his ex-wife Barbara), Rand ended their relationship in 1968 when she discovered he was having another affair with a woman he would later marry. Rand expelled Branden from the movement, announcing their break in an article in the *Objectivist* without mentioning their relationship. They never reconciled.

Rand's life grew more complicated over the following years. She developed lung cancer, the Nathaniel Branden Institute fell apart, and the Collective slowly disintegrated. Rand's husband died in 1979, and she began to reduce her activities. She never completed another novel, though she was working on the notes for one when she died from heart failure and the effects of surgery on her lung cancer and gallstones on March 6, 1982.

About Anthem

Anthem is one of Ayn Rand's earlier works, and presages the fears of collectivism that characterize Objectivism and her later work, such as *The Fountainhead* and *Atlas Shrugged*. The novel is set in the future and has a universal, timeless feel in its characterization of an ideal character's struggle against a monolithic state. Over the course of this relatively short novella, Rand sets the individual against the collective and concludes that the rational celebration of self is the only avenue through which technological and societal progress can occur without the suppression of free will.

Rand wrote *Anthem* in 1937, as a break in her composition of *The Fountainhead*, and she published it in 1938, with a revised and more commonly read version appearing in 1946. As in the case of many contemporary writers of dystopian fiction, such as George Orwell with *Animal Farm*, Rand initially wrote her novel as a warning against Soviet Communism before the end of World War II, but did not receive a popular audience until the Russians were no longer wartime allies of Western Europe and the United States. At the time, some contemporary philosophers still supported the Soviet Union, and even those who saw problems with the regime such as George Orwell believed that less extreme versions such as socialism might still have legitimate value. Rand, on the other hand, rejected all forms of collectivism as inherently flawed, a conclusion that undoubtedly had roots in her experiences in early twentieth-century Russia.

Rand was born in St. Petersburg, Russia, in 1905, the year which marked the defeat of the Russians by the rising military power of the Japanese. In the same year, domestic troubles combined with increasingly bad news abroad sparked a minor revolution -- which proved in many ways a practice run for the future Communist leaders. Twelve years after Rand's birth, the February Revolution caused the abdication of Tsar Nicholas II, and eight months later, Lenin led the Bolsheviks in the October Revolution and wrested power away from the more moderate elements. In the upheaval, Rand's family lost their prosperous business and descended into poverty. Rand became increasingly disgusted with the ill effects of Communism and immigrated to the United States in 1926 after the rise of Stalin in the early 1920s -- but shortly before the purges of the Communist Party and the mass collectivization of agriculture which led to much conflict among the kulaks, or rich peasants.

Unsurprisingly, given her background, Rand was a staunch opponent of Communism before and during the Cold War, and she undoubtedly had the pro-socialist elements of the West in mind as well as some of the more socialist elements of Franklin Delano Roosevelt's New Deal when she wrote *Anthem*. In her view, collectivism led inevitably to the persecution of people with original ideas, as well as to the punishment of the able by forcing them to serve the state. As demonstrated in *Anthem*, Rand believed that too much focus on the state led only to the erasure of human rights, and through Equality 7-2521's search for the Unspeakable Word "I", and through the collectivist naming system, she also echoes the Soviet use of propaganda, particularly via the Agitprop department of the Communist Party. Unlike Orwell, who portrayed the Soviet future of *1984* as suppressive through the use of technology, Rand believed that a collectivist society would regress into a repetition of the Dark Ages, further adding to the dystopian nature of her collectivist state.

In *Anthem*, Equality 7-2521 is the embodiment of many Enlightenment and Industrial Revolution values of individualism and progress. Part of the reason why Ayn Rand's writings have become so popular in American society is because she implicitly celebrates American progress in the Gilded Age of the late nineteenth century as the result of the thirst for knowledge and of the drive of individuals, as well as of the emphasis on the rights of "life, liberty, and the pursuit of happiness" declared in the American Revolution. Equality 7-2521 battles in a mental struggle against the tyranny of the group, and he eventually succeeds against those individuals -- such as the Scholars -- who take the path of least resistance and uphold the collectivist status quo. He is a typical Randian hero, with a hard, strong body and a fearless, proud, and active mind to match, and in the end, he affirms the right to individually driven production.

Character List

Equality 7-2521

A man who has always been too curious and too intelligent for his peers and his society, he finds a secret tunnel where he conducts scientific experiments and rediscovers electricity. He tries to show the World Council of Scholars his electrical invention, but he is forced to run away from the City and is joined by Liberty 5-3000, whom he loves and who calls him "the Unconquered." In the process, he realizes the dangers of collectivism and, upon learning the word "I," renames himself "Prometheus."

Council of Vocations

Three males and two females with white hair and cracked faces who assign Equality 7-2521 the job of Street Sweeper after he leaves the Home of the Scholars.

Union 5-3992

A pale, stupid, and sickly boy who suffers from seizures. When Equality 7-2521 is younger, he tries unsuccessfully to imitate Union 5-3992's dullness, and when the two are older they work in a brigade of Street Sweepers with International 4-8818. Union 5-3992 is too slow to understand Equality 7-2521's contact with Liberty 5-3000.

International 4-8818

A friend of Equality 7-2521, he is a fellow Street Sweeper and has laughter in his eyes. He is too afraid to break the law and join his friend in exploring the secret tunnel, but he is loyal and does not betray Equality 7-2521 and tell the authorities about his friend's use of the tunnel or contact with Liberty 5-3000.

Liberty 5-3000

Referred to by Equality 7-2521 as the Golden One, she is one of the Peasants who till the land outside of the city, but unlike the other women she is tall, beautiful, and proud. She and Equality 7-2521 admit their love for each other, and when he runs away into the Uncharted Forest, she follows him. After they find a home, he renames her Gaea.

Fraternity 2-5503

A Street Sweeper, he is "a quiet boy with wise, kind eyes" who often cries for a reason he cannot understand.

Solidarity 9-6347

A Street Sweeper who is fearless and bright in the daytime but screams "Help us!" in his sleep. His screams unsettle those around him, but the Doctors cannot cure him.

The Transgressor

Also called the Saint of the pyre by Equality 7-2521, he speaks the Unspeakable Word "I" and is burned at the stake. He goes to his death proudly and calmly, and as he dies, he looks at Equality 7-2521 as if to ask Equality 7-2521 to find the Unspeakable Word and be his heir.

Evil Ones

The men from the unmentionable times who had most fully realized a society that celebrated the power of the individual but who were destroyed in the Dawn of the Great Rebirth by the originators of the current collectivist society.

Council of the Home

The men who are in charge of Equality 7-2521's living situation, they tell him that he is happy because he is working for other men, and later they send him to the Palace of Corrective Detention.

Judges

The men who torture and question Equality 7-2521 about his whereabouts at the Palace of Corrective Detention.

Collective 0-0009

The oldest and wisest member of the World Council of Scholars, who rejects Equality 7-2521's present of the glass box and who leads the others in his reprimanding of Equality 7-2521 for his temerity. He announces that the glass box must be destroyed.

World Council of Scholars

The annual meeting of the world's most important scholars, the World Council is actually nothing more than a frightened, intolerant group of men.

Major Themes

Dangers of collectivism

Ayn Rand wrote *Anthem* approximately two decades after the events of the 1917 Russian Revolution, and the ills and misdoings of the Soviet government under Josef Stalin greatly influenced Rand's understanding of the value of collectivism. The USSR had originated from the idea that Communism, an extreme version of socialism, would help the common people by collectivizing many aspects of life. Such collectivist principles assumed that when everyone serves each other according to his ability, then everyone in the society will mutually benefit. However, in Russia, the Communists' rise to power had been bloody and entangled with totalitarian policies in the name of socialism. While many contemporary philosophers claimed the Great Depression's relatively mild impact on the Soviet Union as proof of Communism's efficacy, and others assumed that Soviet Communism had become repressive due to the failings of its leaders, Rand concluded that collectivism had inherent flaws, which she sought to illuminate in *Anthem.*

In Equality 7-2521's society, collectivism has defeated more capitalist societies in the Great Rebirth, and as a result, every aspect of society is integrated into a rigid state system. The school system indoctrinates the state's children with the philosophy that instead of living to satisfy their own desires, they must live exclusively for their brothers, paralleling the Soviet use of "comrade" for fellow citizens. The society is highly dystopian, and Ayn Rand suggests that groups of people never make decisions that are as far-sighted and progressive as those of individuals. Consequently, the society has regressed to the technology of the pre-Enlightenment era, repeating the Dark Age, and men such as Equality 7-2521 who could benefit their society are encouraged to waste their talents. The central thrust of the novella involves Equality 7-2521's search for a philosophy alternative to collectivism and to its emphasis on the group and the state. Eventually Equality 7-2521 rejects all tenants of collectivism. At the same time, as critics have mentioned, a reader of *Anthem* may usefully recall that Rand uses a very extreme form of collectivism to make her point, and that the solution to *Anthem*'s society may be a moderate rather than an entirely individualist society.

Egoism

Otherwise known as individualism, egoism is the philosophy Equality 7-2521 discovers along with the word "I" as the alternative to the damagingly radical altruism of *Anthem.* He learns that although his society has taught him that to be alone is evil and to work for others is good, he must actually work for himself and take pride in his self in order to achieve happiness. Whereas he initially fools himself into believing that he is evil because he is different from his peers, he concludes at the end of the novel that his individuality and his exceptional mental and physical traits actually make him superior and capable. He retains vestiges of his original indoctrination in collectivism until his final break from society at his meeting with the World Council of Scholars, after which he realizes that his reasoning that his glass box is important because of its potential to help his society is merely a justification. In reality, he protects the glass box because, as his creation, it is an extension of his body, and he takes pride in it for its own sake rather than for its use to serve others.

Rand does not specifically use the word "egoism" in *Anthem*, unlike in some of her other works, but Equality 7-2521's actions embody the idea of egoism. Rand dubs it egoism rather than egotism because egotism gives a negative connotation to self-interest, whereas egoism is the celebration of self and the source of happiness. As Equality 7-2521 notes, his society pretends that everyone will be happy in serving their fellow man, but this imposition of a false utopia leads only to fear and slavery for those who are strong and capable. He cites those in history who threw off such chains as role models for the future, and egoism has associations with a number of Enlightenment ideas, especially the rights to "life, liberty, and the pursuit of happiness" which form much of the theoretical basis to the American Constitution.

Freedom versus fear

The contrast between individualism, which leads to freedom, and collectivism, which leads to fear, becomes particularly clear after the Council of the Home reprimands Equality 7-2521 for singing. One of the council members informs him, "Indeed you are happy. How else can men be when they live for their brothers?" In response, Equality 7-2521 realizes that the answer to the council member's question is not as obvious as the authorities have implied. He sees a great deal of contrary evidence among the other Street Sweepers, many of whom presumably received such a lowly job assignment precisely because of their dangerously superior abilities -- and have thus suffered at the hands of collectivism. In particular, he cites Fraternity 2-5503 and Solidarity 9-6347 as men who are afraid of something that they cannot name because they do not have the concepts necessary to express their fear.

Equality 7-2521 is the only person in his society besides Liberty 5-3000 and, to a lesser extent, International 4-8818 who knows how to defeat his fear and be happy. In Equality 7-2521's case, he finds peace and happiness in his scientific work and his pursuit of knowledge and morality. Later, as he discovers happiness even more purely in the Uncharted Forest, his changing emotional states lead him to realize that solitude provides happiness because it also provides freedom. In his tunnel, he has the freedom to think as he wishes, and after he escapes the City, he joyously finds that no one is constraining him and preventing him from fulfilling his deepest desires. Rand suggests that fear is associated with the slavery of collectivism, because in order to shackle the able and the worthy, society must also chain them mentally with fear.

The human spirit

Prometheus and Gaea represent the pinnacles of the human spirit, just as the Unmentionable Times represent the height of human achievement prior to the fall of the Great Rebirth. After learning the Unspeakable Word, Prometheus tells the story of human history as a repeated escape from the tyranny of gods and kings and birthright, which prior to the Great Rebirth paralleled the continual advance of technology, driven by productive individuals. The protagonist's journey from Equality 7-2521 to Prometheus shows that despite the setbacks caused by collectivism, recovery from the Dark Ages is inevitable because of the curiosity and creativity of the rational man. Equality 7-2521 and the Saint of the pyre are both men of great integrity who willingly sacrifice for the sake of freedom and knowledge, and *Anthem* ends on a highly positive note, as the narrator expects to gather like-minded friends to defy the stagnation of their society.

Despite the positive ending of *Anthem*, however, not all humans are portrayed as embodying the best of the human spirit. In contrast to men such as Equality 7-2521 are Union 5-3992 and the men of the World Council of Scholars, who stay within the collectivist system because they feel safer by taking advantage of those who are capable. Rand suggests that although men should all have the same freedoms under the law, not all men are born with equal attributes, and the early inculcation of collectivist beliefs can inculcate men who are already weak into the existing system. Nevertheless, the triumphant ending of *Anthem* indicates that humanity by and large still has outstanding individuals with the will and the ability to bring progress.

Reason versus irrationality

In his experiments in the tunnel, Equality 7-2521 essentially rediscovers the scientific method as he conducts research on electricity and eventually manages to invent an electric light. His rational approach in the tunnel extends to other areas of his life, as he begins to keep a journal in which he ceaselessly questions the tenets of his society and tries to rebuild a philosophical foundation for individualism that disappeared after the Unmentionable Times. He reasons in particular that his society's views regarding the advantages of serving humanity and the state cannot be correct, precisely because none of his obedient coworkers experience happiness more often than fear, and he constantly tries to interpret his own emotional reactions in order to discover an articulate solution to what he instinctively feels is a problem. In this sense and in the sense that only logical thinking can bring technological progress, Equality 7-2521 embodies the benefits of the rationality praised by Objectivism.

In contrast to the activities of Equality 7-2521, the authorities of *Anthem's* collectivist society demonstrate the dangers of illogical reasoning. In the purely scientific area, they propagate the unquestioned belief that the earth is flat and at the center of the galaxy, while bleeding men with leeches is an effective medical treatment. Despite the obvious logical lapses engendered by their scientific views, the Council of Scholars chooses not to question its understanding of the universe, and thus cannot progress away from the collectivist Dark Age. Furthermore, the authorities believe that they can justify collectivism simply by insisting that men are happier while serving others, and even when faced with the triumph of reason when faced with the glass box, the World Council of Scholars choose to reject it based on fear and excuses rather than following the rational path. By juxtaposing Equality 7-2521 with the pettiness of the Council, Rand demonstrates the problems with wishful rather than clear-sighted thinking.

Love and friendship

Along with the pursuit of scientific knowledge and eventually the search for the Unspeakable Word, the development of Equality 7-2521's relationship with the Golden One constitutes one of the major threads of *Anthem*'s plot. At first, Equality 7-2521 reviles the activities at the Palace of Mating because he has no choice in the assignment of his sexual partners, and he believes that his preference for the Golden One is a sin because he is elevating her above all her sisters. However, as he develops in his understanding of the importance of self, he comes to believe that preference and freedom of choice are the basis for happiness, and that the authorities' teaching that men should love all other humans equally merely perpetuates the servitude of collectivism. His friendship with International 4-8818 is the forerunner of his relationship with the Golden One, and alludes to similar themes although the bond is less tight.

For Ayn Rand, love and friendship are not simply an irrational attachment to another human being. Instead, they are the result of the mutual recognition of like-minded individuals, where Equality 7-2521, for example, sees that the Golden One has and fulfills his ideals. For Equality 7-2521, love of another person is the extension of the love of self because he loves her for the same qualities that he loves in himself -- such as fearlessness, integrity, and pride. In the society of his birth, however, people do not learn to love others because collectivism rejects the love of self, and Equality 7-2521's attachment to the Golden One indicates his readiness to move away from such collectivist doctrine.

Thought and language

As an author who chose to propagate the ideals of Objectivism through a work of fiction, Rand recognized the power that words can have on the populace, and she develops the relationship between thought and language throughout *Anthem*. Like her contemporary George Orwell, who also warns of the dystopian possibilities of Communism in *Animal Farm* and *1984*, Rand has her society twist language to serve the purposes of the state. Where *1984* underlines doublethink via such slogans as "War is Peace; Freedom is Slavery; Ignorance is Strength," *Anthem*'s society has completely eliminated the word "I." Consequently, those born within the society grow up without a complete concept of individuality, and whatever remnants of self-awareness remain are discouraged as a sin by the government. These models of twisted language often reflect the Soviet use of propaganda as exemplified by Agitprop, a Communisty Party department strictly devoted to indoctrinating Communist ideals in the Soviet Union.

Even Equality 7-2521, who of all the characters in the book best understands the value of the self, cannot fully comprehend his own philosophy until he ceases to refer to himself as "We" and rediscovers singular pronouns in his language. He and the Golden One also have particular troubles as they repeatedly stumble into confusion because they cannot declare their affection for each other with simplicity and directness. The Golden One's first words to him after he tells her of his discovery of "I" are "I love you," and the statement is not just an affirmation of their love but a declaration of victory in their fight against the teachings of their childhood.

Glossary of Terms

brine

Water mixed with salt (usually table salt) in a solution

collectivism

A society in which the people as a group determine the welfare of the state

ego

Synonym for self

eugenics

Breeding for positive traits in the human race

furrow

In farming, a shallow ditch created in the ground which provides a place for seeds

grill

A dividing screen of metal, often installed on windows or doors

hearth

A fireplace, especially in the sense of being at the center of the home

hedge

A row of shrubs that are close together and thus serve as a barrier

illustrious

Famous and well-regarded

impotent

Incapable; lacking power

loadstone

Also spelled "lodestone," a piece of magnetic rock

manuscript

A written document, often in the sense of being handwritten

pyre

A pile of flammable wood on which a human body is burned

sanction

Official permission

smolder

To burn in a muffled but intense manner

torrent

A chaotic stream

transgression

The committing of a wrong that is against the law or unethical

tunic

A simple, loose type of clothing

vainly

Without the desired success

vocation

The long-term career or job of an individual

Short Summary

Ever since Equality 7-2521 was a child, he has been more physically and mentally vigorous than his classmates, but his collectivist society has taught him that to be different is a sin. He tries unsuccessfully to suppress his curiosity, and for his crime of preference in desiring a position with the wise Scholars, the Council of Vocations assigns him a job as a Street Sweeper. For four years, Equality 7-2521 tries to acquit himself admirably in his vocation and to follow the rigid schedule of his life, but one day, he and International 4-8818 discover a secret tunnel from the Unmentionable Times before the Great Rebirth. International 4-8818 is too afraid to explore, but he is a loyal friend and does not betray Equality 7-2521, who begins to sneak away to conduct scientific experiments in the tunnel. Equality 7-2521 keeps a journal describing his experiences. This in turn forms the book's narrative. Significantly, Equality 7-2521 speaks always as "we" rather than "I", because his society does not have singular pronouns. He desires forgiveness for keeping the tunnel to himself and for thinking the thoughts of an individual rather than of the collective.

One day, as Equality 7-2521 is working in a Street Sweeper's brigade north of the city, he sees and is immediately attracted to the beautiful and proud Liberty 5-3000 among the Peasants. She also notices him, and they greet each other with subtle gestures. Eventually Equality 7-2521 finds an opportunity to speak with Liberty 5-3000 privately, knowing that International 4-8818 will not betray his contact with her. He has privately named her the Golden One, although such a unique name is a sin, and the two clumsily express preference for each other, despite their lack of a sufficient vocabulary to do so. Equality 7-2521 returns home happily, and upon being reprimanded for singing, he reflects on the fear and unhappiness of his coworkers while wondering about the Unmentionable Times and the Unspeakable Word, for which the Transgressor, a heroic man, had been executed at the stake.

After some time, Equality 7-2521 again speaks with the Golden One in the field. She has named him the Unconquered, although this act of individualization is forbidden, and she expresses a willingness to obey him. She brings him water to drink, and the contact between her hands and his lips spurs a new feeling of desire in Equality 7-2521. This confuses him, as he has previously only experienced sex through the indignities of the Palace of Mating.

During Equality 7-2521's private experiments in the tunnel, he rediscovers electricity, which is remarkable in a society that has lost all technology except for the candle, and he realizes that the Council of Scholars may not be as wise and omniscient as he had previously believed. He also concludes from the contents of the tunnel that the men of the Unmentionable Times had also known about electricity, and he decides to continue experimentation, ignoring his worries about breaking the law and finally succeeding in constructing a glass box that emits electric light. He begins to take pride in his own body and his accomplishments, and he decides that he will bring his invention to the upcoming World Council of Scholars, in the hope that it may help his fellow man, exonerate him for his crimes, and thereby allow him to rejoin society.

The day that Equality 7-2521 creates the glass box, he loses track of time and is caught for his absence and sent to the Palace of Corrective Detention for torture. However, he refuses to tell the Judges about his whereabouts in order to protect the light. The day before the meeting of the Council of Scholars, he escapes because the locks are rusted and the doors have no guards. (No one in their brainwashed society has ever thought to escape the Palace before.) He brings his creation to the Council, but rather than rewarding him for his ingenuity, they fear him and his creation and decide to destroy the glass box. To protect his creation, he takes it and escapes blindly through the window into the Uncharted Forest at the edge of the City, realizing in the process that he had actually built the box for himself and not to benefit society.

In spite of his initial despair at his sundering from his community, Equality 7-2521 thoroughly enjoys his first day of true freedom in the Uncharted Forest, reveling in his own strength and ability. In a stream, he sees his reflection for the first time, and he is delighted to see that the beauty of his body matches the worthiness of his mind. To his delight, the Golden One follows him into the Forest, despite her misgivings about being damned, and he teaches her not to suspect corruption in solitude as they have been taught. They begin traveling away from the city, sustaining themselves through the efforts of their bodies. Equality 7-2521 is joyful, and wonders how humanity's thoughts about morality have gone so wrong. At the same time, he and the Golden One wonder about the Unspeakable Word, without which they cannot truly express their love for each other.

Upon exiting the forest, Equality 7-2521 and the Golden One travel across mountains and find a house built in the Unspeakable Times, where they decide to make their home. They are surprised to find that the structure housed only two people, and the Golden One is fascinated by her reflection in the mirrors, while Equality 7-2521 wonders what his heart and nature are trying to tell him as he struggles through the vestiges of his old belief in collectivism. He reads the books in the house's library and discovers that the Unspeakable Word must be "I," representing the concept of the centrality of self that collectivism has removed from the culture.

Triumphantly, Equality 7-2521 explains in his journal that he needs no reason to exist except for himself, and that the error of collectivism was to assume that extreme altruism would free instead of enslave the individual. Only through egoism and the rejection of the worship of "We" can man achieve happiness and pride in his work, and friendship is earned rather than automatically forced on all men. Equality 7-2521 renames himself Prometheus and his wife Gaea, and he plans to raise his son as a free man and to return to the City briefly to gather like-minded men such as International 4-8818. He also decides to rebuild what the Great Rebirth destroyed from the Unmentionable Times, knowing that the power of the individual will ultimately achieve victory over the oppression and stagnation of the group.

Quotes and Analysis

It is a sin to write this. It is a sin to think words no others think and to put them down upon a paper no others are to see. It is base and evil. It is as if we were speaking alone to no ears but our own. And we know well that there is no transgression blacker than to do or think alone.

1.1 (Chapter 1, Paragraph 1)

Equality 7-2521 begins *Anthem* with this declaration of his sins, indicating the degree to which his society has influenced the development of his thoughts. As the quote suggests, he is a potential rebel who has dared to defy the tenets of his society and who will undoubtedly go further on the road to radicalization, but, significantly, he suffers a great deal of guilt as a result. At the same time, the reader sympathizes with him because his "sin" of thinking alone is almost laughably non-criminal and because the potential repercussions are ominously severe. In addition, the narrator speaks in the first-person plural, suggesting that the concept of "I" has disappeared from his society. Thus, the opening lines immediately establish the setting of *Anthem* as a dystopian world, while foreshadowing the main character's inner conflict regarding the relative merits of collectivism and individualism.

What -- even if we have to burn for it like the Saint of the pyre -- what is the Unspeakable Word?

2.57

The Transgressor, or Saint of the pyre, recognizes Equality 7-2521's worth even as he burns, and, with his eyes, he asks Equality 7-2521 to carry on his battle and return the Unspeakable Word to the human language. For his part, Equality 7-2521 recognizes his duty; so is born his obsession with the Unspeakable Word, which he suspects will crystallize all his doubts about his society and provide him with an alternative mode by which to live. Even after he escapes with Liberty 5-3000 from the City and his conflict with his society temporarily comes to a close, Equality 7-2521's search for the Unspeakable Word continues. It is the very embodiment of his quest for understanding.

No single one can possess greater wisdom than the many Scholars who are elected by all men for their wisdom. Yet we can.

3.7

With the discovery of electricity, Equality 7-2521 substantially reevaluates his idolization of the Home of the Scholars for the first time. Whereas he used to believe that he could research nature best by working collectively with the other Scholars, he now questions the efficacy of the group when, by himself, he has achieved more than the previous century of Scholars. This development marks a crucial step in his evolution away from the collectivist principles he has learned from his society, and it underlines Rand's principle that, because groups are held back by their lowest common denominators, only individuals can drive progress. Equality 7-2521 admits to some struggles against this point of view, but he sees no other possible conclusion, and his eventual reinvention of the electric light only serves to confirm it.

For this wire is a part of our body, as a vein torn from us, glowing with our blood. Are we proud of this thread of metal, or of our hands which made it, or is there a line to divide these two?

5.10

This passage marks a new step in the development of Equality 7-2521's break with his collectivist society, as he begins to ignore the conventional rejection of self awareness. Before, he has never particularly cared about his own body, but now that he has created the glass box, he takes pride in his accomplishment and associates the powers of his mind with the powers of his body. In Rand's view, the celebration of the body is akin to the celebration of the individual, and Equality 7-2521 describes the electrical wire as an extension of his self. He begins to love his creation not because of its potential use for others but because its existence is a memorial to his power as an individual, although he has not yet clarified this in his own mind.

Our blessing upon you, our brothers! Tomorrow, you will take us back into your fold and we shall be an outcast no longer. Tomorrow we shall be one of you again. Tomorrow . . .

6.28

Despite Equality 7-2521's torture at the hands of the Judges of the Palace of Corrective Detention and despite his new ideas regarding the abilities of the individual, his determination to show his box to the World Council of Scholars shows that he still believes in some major tenets of collectivism. Most importantly, he has been taught that solitude is a crime and a corrupting influence, and he still deeply desires to end his mental isolation from his society. He displays some degree of the illogical thinking displayed by other members of his community because he hopes too optimistically and without any legitimate basis that the World Council of Scholars will embrace him and have his vocation changed. Wishful thinking has deluded him, but his meeting with the World Council will soon dash those illusions him and force him irretrievably on the path away from the City's mores.

We have lied to ourselves. We have not built this box for the good of our brothers. We built it for its own sake.

As Equality 7-2521 sleeps on the moss inside the Uncharted Forest, he suffers a moment of disillusionment and despair, but the pain of his recent detachment from his society forces a recognition of his lie to himself. He has told himself that he loves his glass box because of its potential for society's benefit, but, in reality, he cherishes it because it was the product of his own ingenuity and rationality and because it is thus an extension of his self. This understanding of his own motivations is essential for him to continue his discovery of Objectivist and individualist principles, as he must cut all ties with the false precepts of collectivism in order to truly understand what makes him happy. His society has informed him that he must be happy because he serves others, but he and other men are only truly happy when they can work as they wish for themselves.

Our face was not like the faces of our brothers, for we felt no pity when looking upon it. Our body was not like the bodies of our brothers, for our limbs were straight and thin and hard and strong.

8.7

For the first time in his life, Equality 7-2521 sees his own reflection. (The City does not have mirrors or streams such as this one, for fear that they might reinforce vanity and promote individualism.) Ayn Rand treats a moderate level of vanity as a positive sign of self-interest, and, accordingly, Equality 7-2521 is proud of his image. He is the prototypical and ideal man, and as a result, his mind and his body are both extensions of his self and of each other. Consequently, his body reflects his personal characteristics of strength and fearlessness, and these traits are the same qualities that he sees and so admires in the Golden One. For both Equality 7-2521 and the Golden One, the body does not contrast with the mind in any form, and as a result, their selves are portrayed as complete and without contradiction.

"We are one . . . alone . . . and only . . . and we love you who are one . . . alone . . . and only."

We looked into each other's eyes and we knew that the breath of a miracle had touched us, and fled, and left us groping vainly.

9.38-39

Here, the Golden One attempts to explain that she loves Equality 7-2521, but she clearly lacks the necessary vocabulary to do so, and the failed attempt leaves both of them immensely frustrated. They do not know the Unspeakable Word "I," and because of this, they feel instinctively that they are missing an essential concept in their understanding of the world. Love, in the world of *Anthem*, is an expression of the kinship of two selves, but without the fully articulated expression of self, they cannot verbally consummate their love. The issue of vocabulary rears its head earlier as well, when the lovers meet by the hedge and try to explain their mutual attraction -- this time by stating that they do not wish to be siblings. Fittingly, once Equality 7-2521 deciphers the Unspeakable Word in his books, the Golden One's first words to him are "I love you" -- signaling the completion of his quest.

I am. I think. I will.

11.1

These three brief and rhythmically intense sentences open the penultimate chapter of *Anthem*, after Equality 7-2521 has finally fulfilled his search for the Unspeakable Word. Speaking hereafter in the first-person singular rather than the first-person plural, which he emphasizes by using "I" or "me" in nearly every sentence of the chapter, he finds that he has found the answer for his existence not in humanity but in himself and in each individual man. What he refers to as the "worship of the word 'We'" has caused the deterioration of human society from the pinnacle of millennia of technological achievement into a second Dark Age, but he now knows the way to end this stagnation and restart the ascent of mankind. As suggested by these sentences, he and his mind and will are the only real motivations, and Chapter Eleven is his manifesto of freedom and self-worth -- a manifesto rejects living for others as mere servitude.

And here, over the portals of my fort, I shall cut in the stone the word which is to be my beacon and my banner. The word which will not die, should we all perish in battle. The word which can never die on this earth, for it is the heart of it and the meaning and the glory.

The sacred word:

EGO

12.25-26

Ayn Rand's original title for *Anthem* was *Ego*, and so it is appropriate that the sacred word ego is the culmination of Prometheus's physical and philosophical journey through the novella. His plans to cut the word "ego" in stone stands in contrast to the words cut in marble at the beginning of the book -- words that declare that "there are no men but only the great WE" and are the antithesis of Prometheus's final conclusion. He calls "ego" his banner, suggesting that he has essentially declared a holy war on collectivism, where his deity is not a god but rather an idea. He also labels ego a beacon, a choice of words that reflects Rand's emphasis on light and human progress throughout her story. Prometheus has resurrected "ego" and consequently believes that it is an immortal concept, one which will remain as long as worthy men continue to be born; likewise, he associates the concept with nature, which had guided him so faithfully to his discovery of "I."

Summary and Analysis of Chapter One

Summary:

Always speaking from a first-person plural point of view, the narrator introduces himself as Equality 7-2521. He explains that the act of keeping a secret journal without the permission of the Council of Vocations is against the law and a sin because his thoughts are not shared, but personal. However, he has committed an even greater crime. He is writing alone in a tunnel with a stolen candle, although the laws require that no one can ever be alone, and he describes himself as twenty-one years old and six feet tall. His height has made him stand out from his peers, hinting at his evil tendency to think unlike others in spite of the efforts of the World Council to unite all men and reject individuality. The Council's creed of unity has been written on their palace since the Great Rebirth ended the selfish Unmentionable Times, the study of which is forbidden and will also send Equality 7-2521 to the Palace of Corrective Detention.

Equality 7-2521 recalls the life that led him to his worst crime, beginning with his early years in the Home of Infants. The narrative switches temporal registers, and we learn of this childhood -- one spent largely in a sleeping hall of one hundred beds, one peppered with fights with other children and frequent chastisement. From the ages of five to fifteen, Equality 7-2521 lives at the Home of the Students and there recites a creed every night with the other students before going to bed. The creed declares that the individual is nothing when compared to the group and the State.

Equality 7-2521 does not enjoy his schooling because he is too intelligent for the subject matter and thus stands out from his classmates. He tries unsuccessfully to act like the slow-witted Union 5-3992 and is often punished for his differences. However, he believes in the Teachers because they have been appointed by the just and powerful Council, and he feels guilty because he wants a specific job after the end of his schooling, although he should accept the wisdom of the Council of Vocations.

He has always preferred science and, to the Teachers' dismay, asks too many questions about the subject. The Council of Scholars states that the world is flat and at the center of the galaxy, and the schools teach how to bleed men to cure them; Equality 7-2521 wants to know more and dares to wish for a work assignment to the Home of the Scholars. The Home of the Scholars is the source of all inventions, such as glass and the candle, the latter of which had only been discovered a hundred years ago, and Equality 7-2521 wants to join their investigations. When the Council of Vocations announces their assigned vocations, Equality 7-2521 hopes to be made a Scholar even more than a Leader, an honorable profession which leads to election to the City, State, and World Councils. Instead, he is given the profession of Street Sweeper, and he decides to atone for his sin of desire by proudly working his new job.

As a Street Sweeper, Equality 7-2521 lives by a strict daily schedule, and, before their daily visits to the City Theatre to watch plays about work and duty, the Street Sweepers meet with other men at a Social Meeting in the City Hall, where the Leaders give speeches and the men sing hymns about equality and collectivism. Equality 7-2521 lives in this manner for four years, knowing that at age forty, he will be sent to the retirement Home of the Useless as an Old One or, if he lives past forty-five, an Ancient One. He works in a three-person brigade with Union 5-3992 and International 4-8818, the latter of whom is too full of laughter and thus was assigned to the Street Sweepers instead of the Artists. International 4-8818 is the friend of Equality 7-2521, although they are by law not allowed to admit it.

Two years prior to the writing of his journal, Equality 7-2521 is working beside International 4-8818 because Union 5-3992 is sick with convulsions, and the two discover the iron grill entrance to a tunnel among the weeds next to the City Theatre. Equality 7-2521 decides to explore it, although International 4-8818 opts to stay because he suspects that it is against the law. As Equality 7-2521 investigates the darkness, he realizes that the tunnel must be from the technologically advanced Unmentionable Times. He knows that the Unmentionable Times were horrible, but he still wishes to know more about them.

When Equality 7-2521 returns to the surface, International 4-8818 asks him to report their discovery to the City Council for a reward, but Equality 7-2521 insists on keeping it for himself, knowing that International 4-8818 will not betray his friend (which, after all, would likely earn Equality 7-2521 a death sentence). Afterward, Equality 7-2521 begins to sneak away to the tunnel instead of watching the plays at the City Theatre. With stolen objects and other local materials, he conducts experiments at night, and, with the help of stolen manuscripts, he learns many new things and feels no regret for his curiosity and his transgressions of the law.

Analysis:

Anthem's setting is that of an unclearly defined dystopian society which exists after what Equality 7-2521 calls the Great Rebirth and the end of the Unmentionable Times, an era that appears to be our own. The first paragraph establishes the sinister nature of the society, as the narrator castigates himself for breaking the law by daring to keep a journal. The mention of a Council of Vocations that controls when man can and cannot write also immediately indicates the oppression and jurisdiction over thought in Equality 7-2521's world. Throughout the first chapter, Equality 7-2521 offers no specifics of location that might place him in a particular continent or region, lending a universal feel to the dangers of his society, a sense that is further emphasized by the presence of a "World Council". At the same time, Rand's story has a clear connection to the contemporary political situation, as she wrote the novel partly as a parable to warn about the dangers of Russian Communism and the collectivist philosophy which many major thinkers had at one point in time believed to be a boon for human society.

                                              Summary and Analysis of Chapter One

Although Equality 7-2521 himself expresses guilt rather than awareness of the injustices of his government, he consistently receives punishment from his society for his exceptional qualities, which range from his above-average height of six feet to his intelligence and curiosity regarding the sciences. Because he cannot conform and because he dares to think as an individual rather than as one of the crowd, the Council of Vocations takes away his freedom of choice and makes him a Street Sweeper rather than a Scholar (or, for that matter, any position in which he might make full use of his abilities). The House of Street Sweepers appears to act as a repository for two categories of men -- those such as Union 5-3992 who are too weak or dull for any other job, and those such as Equality 7-2521 and International 4-8818 who are too talented to risk having a more powerful niche in society.

Equality 7-2521 shows only a nascent awareness of his ill treatment at the hands of his collectivist community, indicating that society has successfully enforced conformity in the mental as well as the physical and governmental spheres. As in many dystopian novels of the period -- such as *1984* -- and as in the Soviet Union itself, language becomes a major vehicle through which the society enforces mental compliance. In particular, although Equality 7-2521 narrates *Anthem* from a first-person point of view, he uses the unorthodox first-person plural form "we" rather than the singular "I." Rand suggests that the collectivist use of language represents an entire viewpoint which is ironically more sinful than all of Equality 7-2521's purported crimes. In addition, Rand names the various Councils in a manner reminiscent of the Councils and Ministries of the Soviet Union.

Because of the brainwashing that characterizes the world of *Anthem*, the conflict in the novel has a dual nature. In one sense, Equality 7-2521 is an innovator in an emerging conflict with the stagnant status quo of his society, as he begins to defy the authorities by exploring the tunnel and by keeping it for himself so that he might conduct experiments underground; this conflict appears in turn poised to become more significant as the novel continues. At the same time, Equality 7-2521 is in conflict with himself, as his individualist nature collides with the culture of compliance that has raised him for over twenty years. The antagonist is in both cases an aspect of collectivism, but Equality 7-2521 faces physical obstacles in the first case and mental ones in the second case. Interestingly, the conventions of good and evil are reversed not only in the societal definitions of sin but also in the portrayal of black and white. Whereas white is normally the color of innocence and purity, here it appears most prominently in the oppressive sleeping halls, while black is associated with the freedom of the dark tunnel.

Rand thus far presents Equality 7-2521 as the only truly outstanding individual in his city, but International 4-8818 serves as an example of a worthy man who does not quite have the qualities necessary to engage in a struggle with the oppression of collectivism. As Equality 7-2521's foil, he shares some of the protagonist's creativity and skill, but whereas Equality 7-2521 has a serious nature and prefers the sciences, International 4-8818 has "laughter in his eyes" and apparently has some skill as an artist. Both have suffered because the Council of Vocations deemed them too capable for their true vocations, but International 4-8818 is afraid of punishment and refuses to explore the tunnel with Equality 7-2521. Nevertheless, his loyalty and ability to maintain a friendship in defiance of the law make him a valuable, if not entirely admirable, character.

Summary and Analysis of Chapter Two

Summary:

When working with the Street Sweepers in a road north of the city, Equality 7-2521 sees Liberty 5-3000, a woman from the Home of the Peasants, and he is instantly attracted to her tall, blonde beauty and her fearless, guiltless expression. He learns her name as she is called back to the fields by the others, and he begins to look forward to seeing her every day, although he knows that he is forbidden to express preference for one woman. One day, Liberty 5-3000 also turns to look at him with her taut, severe face before walking away. The next day, Liberty 5-3000 smiles at him, and they begin to greet each other every morning at the hedge between the road and the fields. They do so silently, with a subtle salute, because neither of them is allowed to communicate with those of other vocations.

Equality 7-2521 knows that, for the second time in his life, he is guilty of expressing a preference. Nevertheless, he feels better in Liberty 5-3000's presence. He names her the Golden One because she is not like the others, although it is a sin to bear a unique name, and he also ignores the prohibition against thinking of members of the opposite gender outside of the Time of Mating. For two years, he has been sent once per year to the City Palace of Mating, as have all men over twenty and women over eighteen, but the process of mating with a woman assigned by the Council of Eugenics is shameful, and the parents never see their children.

Eventually, Equality 7-2521 speaks to the Golden One on a day when the other Peasants and Street Sweepers are far away. She rises from kneeling at the moat and walks to the hedge, and, because Equality 7-2521 decides that International 4-8818 will not betray him and that Union 5-3992 will not understand the significance of their conversation, he tells her that she is beautiful. She does not move but reveals a triumphant expression before asking his name.

Liberty 5-3000 then tells Equality 7-2521 that she does not wish him to be her brother, and he says she is not his sister, and although they do not have the vocabulary to explain their attraction, they both understand the meaning of their conversation. She asks if he would look for her even among a multitude of women, and he says he would. He tells her that his brigade of Street Sweepers always works in the same place, and she tells him that his eyes are different from those of others. Liberty 5-3000 tells Equality 7-2521 that she is seventeen, which relieves him, because she has therefore not yet been to the Palace of Mating. He decides to prevent her from being sent to the palace, although he is not sure why this desire is so important to him. She sees his sudden hatred for other men and smiles sadly before she walks away to join three of her sister Peasants. He sees that her hand is trembling as she scatters the seeds.

Equality 7-2521 walks happily back to the Home of the Street Sweepers and is reprimanded for absent-mindedly singing without reason in the dining hall. The member of the Home Council doing the scolding tells Equality 7-2521 that he is right to be happy because he is living for his brothers; Equality 7-2521, however, privately realizes that although the people of his society are not allowed to be unhappy, they are never truly *happy*, but rather just afraid. He is also afraid when among the Street Sweepers, but in his tunnel, where no other men are around, he loses his fear and finds enough strength to seemingly last him the rest of his life. The Council of the Home is suspicious of his joy, but he decides that he is glad to be alive, although he sees Fraternity 2-5503, who cries without reason, and Solidarity 9-6347, who screams in his sleep. No one dares to say what they think as they go to bed, lest their thoughts be too original, but Equality 7-2521 still sees peace and dignity in the sky.

He often thinks about the Uncharted Forest beyond the plains outside the city. He has heard about the occasional man who runs into the Uncharted Forest and never returns, dying of hunger or from wild animals, although the Councils claim this story to be a legend. The Uncharted Forests are said to have grown over the ruins of the Unmentionable Times, and he wonders about the legends of fighting that occurred, when the Evil Ones were conquered and their written words burned in the Script Fire at the Dawn of the Great Rebirth. He wonders what words have been lost with the Unmentionable Times, although he knows it is a sin to wish to know the answer.

In particular, he knows of an Unspeakable Word, and he knows that to speak it is the only crime with a death penalty. At the age of ten, he saw a man burned alive in public for saying the word. The Transgressor's tongue was cut out, but he was young and tall and walked proudly to the stake, smiling as he died. Equality 7-2521 had thought that he was a Saint, and he saw the Transgressor's eyes looking directly at him, begging him to regain the Unspeakable Word. Now, years later, Equality 7-2521 wishes he knew the Word, even if it means death.

Analysis:

Whereas Rand's antagonists are indistinct committee members without a prominent physical presence, she characterizes her protagonists by a distinctly noticeable physical perfection as well as mental superiority. Like Equality 7-2521 and, to a lesser extent, International 4-8818, Liberty 5-3000 is tall and strong, reflecting her fearless stoicism and implying her heroism. Although the Council of Vocations has assigned her a position as a Peasant for the same reasons that they gave the job of Street Sweeper to Equality 7-2521 and International 4-8818, she defies her environment by her stance and mere existence. Through her depiction of Liberty 5-3000, Rand again reverses conventional ideas of what is good by rejecting collectivism as too soft and tame while praising individualism as prideful and hard.

Liberty 5-3000 is Rand's archetypal woman and acts as the female foil to Equality 7-2521 in her strength and integrity. She righteously scorns all that does not deserve her but needs only minimal conversation to intuitively recognize Equality 7-2521's worthiness. Liberty 5-3000 comes to him "as if they [Liberty 5-3000] had heard a command in our [Equality 7-2521's] eyes," suggesting that Rand's ideal of femininity also contains an element of obedience, albeit only to a worthy man. Rand's depiction of the relationship between the dominant male and the ideal but appropriately submissive woman also appears in *The Fountainhead* and *Atlas Shrugged*, and has led to disapproval from some feminists, particularly since this idealized woman is a heroic but two-dimensional character when compared to the fully fleshed description of, say, Equality 7-2521's psyche.

Equality 7-2521 renames Liberty 5-3000 "the Golden One," which both sets her apart as an individual and implicitly critiques the slogan-like numerical designations of their society. Whereas "the Golden One" is a sincere, unique appellation, the numbers in "Liberty 5-3000" and "Equality 7-2521" have a collectivist meaning, where each person is merely one replaceable digit out of many. While in many cases the first word of the collectivist names have a positive connotation, the names are also ironic. Equality 7-2521 is actually more than equal to his peers and is consequently forcibly made equal by the law; Liberty 5-3000, likewise, is not as free as her proud demeanor or name suggest.

As indicated by the Home Council's reprimanding of Equality 7-2521 when he sings, the society of *Anthem* exerts an iron control over the voices of its people. Equality 7-2521 and the Golden One are unable to talk at length, and when they attempt to express their mutual attraction, they do not have the vocabulary to say more than that they do not wish to be siblings. Nevertheless, Equality 7-2521 understands that the freedom of choice is integral to true happiness, while the absence of freedom is fear. He abhors his time in the Palace of Mating because there he has an assigned partner; as a result, he also does not know the concept of jealousy, which is why he finds it difficult to explain to himself why he cares about the Golden One's presence in the Palace of Mating. Simultaneously, when the Council of the Home tells him that he must be happy, he recognizes that because his brothers have no choice in the matter, they are instead afraid and dissatisfied.

Foreshadowing Equality 7-2521's future break with his society are his twin obsessions with the Unmentionable Times and the Unspeakable Word. His assertion that the Council of Scholars had invented the candle one hundred years ago suggests that collectivism has reigned over a long period of stagnation, but the Old Ones as mentioned in the beginning of the novel seem to have some recollection of cars and skyscrapers, and the society's relatively short expected life-span -- forty to fifty years -- suggests that the Great Rebirth was a relatively recent occurrence. Equality 7-2521 feels guilty about wanting to know more about the Evil One's society, but he continues to wonder about the Unspeakable Word, for which the Transgressor, or Saint of the pyre, became a martyr. The Saint's pride and happiness suggest that he had found freedom in the Unspeakable Word, and, via his gaze, he seemed to recognize Equality 7-2521's inherent worth with the same instinctive accuracy as displayed by the Golden One.

Summary and Analysis of Chapter Three

Summary:

Equality 7-2521 announces that in his experiments he has discovered a new aspect of nature. Although he might be punished for his thoughts, he has begun to realize that the Council of Scholars does not know everything that is to be known. Only those who look for nature's secrets are able to find them.

Equality 7-2521 does not know the origins of the particular power he has discovered, but, when he experiments on a dead frog, he sees its leg jerking. After many experiments, he finds that the copper wire on which the frog hangs has somehow combined with the metal in his knife to create the leg jerk. He puts a piece of copper and a piece of zinc into a jar of salty water and connects them with a wire to create this new power.

He is fascinated by what he has discovered, and sees that it defies all the currently known laws of nature. He has been taught by his society that lodestones in compasses always point north, but now he sees that the new power makes the needle of a compass move. He also discovers that, in thunderstorms, if he puts a tall iron rod next to the entrance of the tunnel, the iron will draw the lightning. He reasons that the new power causes lightning -- a radically new notion.

Armed with his new discovery, Equality 7-2521 finds copper wires and boxes with strands of metal from the half-mile of tunnel that is accessible to him between two cave-ins. He also finds wires that lead to glass globes that contain thin threads of metal, and he concludes that people in the Unmentionable Times must have known about this power from the sky. He decides that he must learn more, although he is frightened because no one but he knows about it. For some reason, he knows more than all the Scholars combined, even though they were elected for their knowledge, and he decides that he does not care about breaking the law in order to learn.

Analysis:

With his discovery of electricity, Equality 7-2521 reaches a turning point in his understanding of his society. Whereas his previous ambition was to join the Home of Scholars, he sees that he can accomplish more alone than can the combined intelligence of all the Scholars. For the first time, he begins to comprehend that he might be superior not just to many of his peers but also to those whom he previously idolized as the holders of all knowledge. With this new discovery, his guilt and need for forgiveness from the Councils slowly fade away, although he has not yet become entirely radicalized in his thinking.

When describing his observation of the effects of electricity, Equality 7-2521 says that he "followed in preference to all our studies." He uses the word "preference" without further comment, indicating that he ceases to see the crime of preference as a real moral issue. In *Anthem*, vocabulary is an important motif that can encompass entire cultures and bodies of philosophical thought, and Equality 7-2521's blasé use of a nominally sinful word that formerly worried him is echoed in his increasingly harsh rhetoric about his society. He refers to the Council of Scholars as "blind", whereas before he wrote that they "know all things." As later chapters show, however, he does not yet condemn the Council of Scholars, although he recognizes that he has surpassed them.

As in her other major novels, namely *The Fountainhead* and *Atlas Shrugged*, Rand here juxtaposes the idea of the singular, productive man against the inefficacy of committees. Similarly to Howard Roark's crusade against the stultification of group think in *The Fountainhead*, Equality 7-2521 is the independent individual etched in sharp relief against the collective entity of the Council of the Scholars -- a group that falsely claims the invention of the candle and has made no advances since the Great Rebirth. Instead, Equality 7-2521 sees that he gains knowledge from the actions of his self, and he characteristically records both what he knows and what he does not yet understand. Whereas the Council of Scholars displays no understanding of self and claims that what they do not understand simply does not exist, Rand's protagonist displays a keen awareness of self versus the unknown.

In his underground tunnel, Equality 7-2521 replicates the frog experiments of Luigi Galvani, the battery-creating endeavors of Alessandro Volta, and the lightning research of Benjamin Franklin. These men are comparable in that they all contributed to the study of electricity during the Age of Enlightenment, a period famous for its celebration of and achievements in science and philosophy. By contrast, in the timeline of *Anthem*, these men are all part of the Unmentionable Times, and Equality 7-2521 is forced to hide his discovery from society lest he be punished. The mention of Franklin is particularly important because Franklin was also involved in the American Revolution; he thus helped create Ayn Rand's second country and a major wellspring of the ideals of which Equality 7-2521 has been deprived.

Equality 7-2521's rapid advances in the area of electricity are somewhat unrealistic, given that he has received an inadequate education from the Home of the Students and that he would have to be exceptionally intelligent to match the achievements of three disparate and well-educated men of the Enlightenment. However, he acts as the prototypical man of action and experimentation, and he chooses to seek truth in nature rather than in his society. His investigations are for the sake of knowledge rather than inherently to serve other men, and he represents the spirit of human ingenuity that will ultimately defeat the obstructionist Dark Age collectivism has created. At the same time, the references to the Enlightenment reminds the reader of the tragic loss caused by the Great Rebirth.

                                             Summary and Analysis of Chapter Three

Summary and Analysis of Chapter Four

Summary:

After much time has passed, on a hot day when the Peasants are weary and work far away from the road, Equality 7-2521 sees a second opportunity to speak with Liberty 5-3000, the Golden One. She is waiting at the hedge, and although her eyes are "hard and scornful" toward others, she seems ready to obey Equality 7-2521's words. He tells her that he has named her the Golden One in his thoughts, and she tells him that she has also given him a name -- the Unconquered.

Equality 7-2521 is silent for a moment before he points out that their thoughts are forbidden. She notes that he nevertheless wants her to continue thinking these thoughts, and he does not deny it, causing her to smile. He says: "Our dearest one, do not obey us." She steps back, her eyes wide, and, ignoring his command, she asks him to call her "our dearest one" again. He readily obliges, thinking as he does that no man has ever said such a thing to a woman before.

The Golden One's head bows, and she stands still before Equality 7-2521 with her palms turned toward him, clearly indicating that she is submitting her body to his. He is unable to speak, but she raises her head and soothingly tells him that he must be hot and tired. He disagrees, but she suggests that he come to the cooler fields and drink some water. When he says that he cannot cross the hedge, although he is thirsty, she kneels by the moat and brings water to his lips with her cupped hands. She keeps those hands by his lips even, after he is done drinking. He raises his head and steps back, confused because he does not understand his own actions. She does the same and leaves, walking backward with her arms still bent, as though they were still holding water.

Analysis:

At this point in the novel, Equality 7-2521's relationship with the Golden One has become a major plot strand, and it serves as a second impetus (in addition to the experiments in the tunnel) for Equality 7-2521's development of a sense of self. For these two lovers, love is not just a matter of passionate attraction but the natural and automatic result of a deep kinship in their values, independence, and spirit. In some sense, the most important aspect of Equality 7-2521's love is that he admires himself and thus clearly must admire the Golden One, who is an extension of his self. His friendship with International 4-8818 is a lesser expression of this corollary of the love of self. By contrast, those in his society who have not learned to love themselves cannot experience love for others and are limited to the thoroughly loveless activities at the Palace of Mating.

Just as Equality 7-2521 renames Liberty 5-3000, she changes his name to the Unconquered; the lovers exchange these names, and Equality 7-2521 calls Liberty

5-3000 "our dearest one," underlining the lovers' possession of each other as well as their increasing willingness to commit transgressions against the law through language. Their mutual naming also has religious overtones, and as the story progresses, Equality 7-2521 and Liberty 5-3000 begin to resemble renderings of the first man and first woman in many world religions and mythologies.

Further religious imagery appears as the Golden One offers Equality 7-2521 water from the moat. Her gesture of placing her wet hands next to his lips is reminiscent both of an offering and a baptism. Equality 7-2521 and the Golden One continue to act as the representative man and woman, pantomiming a ritual of desire and of individual, selfish love. They do not yet entirely understand the feeling of sexual attraction, echoing the state of Adam and Eve as they began in Eden. Ayn Rand intended for the writing of *Anthem* to be somewhat archaic, and her early drafts of *Anthem* reveal more direct references to phrases from the Bible, indicating her awareness of the parallels in her own archetypal couple.

In offering the water to Equality 7-2521, the Golden One combines the traditional female roles as a mother-like caregiver and an obedient wife. Equality 7-2521 observes that she obeys him because she considers him worthy; he tells her not to obey him, but she ironically insists upon submitting to his authority. A feminist reading of *Anthem* might well find this to be problematic. On the one hand, the Golden One is a capable and heroic individual in her own right, and Rand does not portray her as spiritually inferior to Equality 7-2521. However, the power relationship between the two is not equal, as Equality 7-2521 never proclaims his obedience to her, and the traditionally parochial view of male and female roles is largely preserved as Equality 7-2521 acts and the Golden One supports. Even more unsettling is the view suggested by *The Fountainhead*, in which Howard Roark's rape of Dominique Francon is portrayed positively, as a battle of wills in which the hero forces the heroine to submit, again reinforcing gender roles in a troubling manner.

The setting of Chapter Four is the hedge separating the Peasants' fields and the road leading to the city, on a particularly hot and oppressive day. Ironically, the heat that takes away the spirit and energy of the other women in the field allows the Golden One to escape the repressive laws and speak with Equality 7-2521 without being overheard. The hedge is a symbol of separation, representing the rules that prevent the two lovers from permanently joining, but it also represents the border between the city and its outer limits. As Equality 7-2521 approaches the border to talk to the Golden One, he also approaches the figurative border that will eventually lead to his break with his society.

Summary and Analysis of Chapter Five

Summary:

Equality 7-2521 is stunned because he has created something new by himself. After countless days and failed attempts, he has managed to use the artifacts from the Unmentionable Times to construct a glass box which can harness his previously discovered power of the sky. Whenever he connects wires to the box and closes the current, the wire glows in a circle of light. He is amazed because it shines light without the help of a fire.

He blows out the candle and can see his fingers against the wire's red light, and he becomes unaware of anything except for his hands above the light. He realizes that he can now light his tunnel as well the Cities and thus give everyone a new, cleaner, and brighter light. Man can harness the power to his will, and he knows that he must not keep his secret to himself and continue working only at night. He wants to join the other Scholars in finding new aspects of his discovery.

In a month, the World Council of Scholars is coming to their annual meeting, and this particular meeting will be in his city. He decides to gift the Council with his invention and confess everything, believing that they will forgive him for his transgressions. Then, he imagines, the Council of Scholars will have the Council of Vocations reassign him to the Home of the Scholars, even though reassignment never occurs.

Equality 7-2521 decides to wait until the World Council and guard his tunnel, knowing that if anyone other than a Scholar were to find the secret, that person will not understand the significance of the glass box. Instead, Equality 7-2521 and his light will be destroyed because of his crime. For the first time, he cares not only about the light but about his own survival, because his body and his invention are connected. He stretches his arms, feeling their power, and he suddenly wishes to know the details of his own appearance, although it is evil to look at his own body or ask others about it.

Analysis:

In Rand's original drafts of *Anthem*, she opened the paragraph describing Equality 7-2521's invention of a primitive light bulb in a different manner: "The Light! . . . Here, under our hands, at our bidding, the light of the sky, the light to set the earth aglow, the Light smokeless and flameless and unquenchable!" (qtd. in Mayhew 35). The revised version states more succinctly, "We made it. We created it. We brought it forth from the night of the ages. We alone. Our hands. Our mind. Ours alone and only," thus shifting the emphasis away from the invention of the light itself and more closely to the achievement of Equality 7-2521. Similarly, she decapitalizes "the Light," and, in its stead, she equates light with the more basic idea of self.

The chapter marks the height of the first crescendo of optimism and exuberance in *Anthem*'s narrative arc. If Chapter Three recounted Equality 7-2521's rediscovery of Enlightenment principles, then Equality 7-2521's achievements in this section clearly echo the work of Thomas Edison, the prolific American inventor of the first practical light bulb. He consequently moves from the Enlightenment era to the period of the Industrial Revolution, further pulling out of the mental Dark Age of his rearing. He observes the light within the context of darkness, and he experiments with the glass box in order to provide a glimpse of knowledge in a world that has lost much of its technology and understanding of nature. In a feat of human ingenuity, he does so in an extremely oppressive environment.

Although Equality 7-2521's invention of the glass box is in part remarkable because he arrives at it without any support from society, Rand depicts him as succeeding because of as well as in spite of his lonely surroundings. The creation of the light causes him to be aware of and take pride in the strength of his own body, and the glass box becomes the emblem of his self-love. He concludes the chapter by wishing to know about his own appearance because he suspects correctly that his body reflects his inner strength and superiority, much as the Golden One's exterior exhibits her heroic qualities.

Despite the reinforcement to Equality 7-2521's sense of ego through the construction of the glass box, he has not entirely freed himself of the paradigms of his civilization. He no longer feels guilty about sneaking away and personally working toward his own achievement, but he still believes to some extent in his culture's doctrine that all work should be for the purpose of serving others. He rationalizes the discrepancy between his discovery and his society's morality by explaining that his invention is important because it will serve all of humanity. He is correct, but events later in the novel will cause him to understand that he values the light first for its own sake as the result of his production and only second as a herald of technology.

While still exulting in the value his self, Equality 7-2521 nevertheless does not continue to think of his experimentation as a solitary affair. Instead, he dreams of being welcomed into the Home of the Scholars and joining with them in a cooperative effort to develop more uses of electricity. This remaining vestige of Equality 7-2521's belief in collectivism could serve as a hooking point which will contain the danger he poses to his dystopian communist society. However, the fear and shortsightedness inherent in collectivism will prevent them from accepting him and thus ending his radicalization.

Summary and Analysis of Chapter Six

Summary:

Equality 7-2521 is unable to write for thirty days after his decision to bring his invention to the World Council of Scholars because he is caught. He is absorbed in his thoughts that he forgets to watch the time and return to the City Theatre. He hastens to the Theatre, but it is too late, and he returns to the Home of the Street Sweepers.

When he speaks to the Council of the Home, he thinks of his glass box and of its light and refuses to tell them of his whereabouts. The oldest member of the Council is incurious and in a bored voice has the youngest members send Equality 7-2521 to the Palace of Corrective Detention for interrogation. Equality 7-2521 goes to the windowless Stone Room of the Palace of Corrective Detention, where he sees an iron post and two men who wear only leather aprons and hoods.

The Councilmember escorts leave Equality 7-2521 to the two Judges in the corner of the room. The Judges, who are "small, thin men, grey and bent," have the hooded men take off Equality 7-2521's clothes and tie his hands to the iron post. Kneeling, Equality 7-2521 does not cry out, although the numerous lashes on his back are extremely painful, and he stares at the door's iron grill while thinking of the square stones on the wall and the squares of lacerations on his back.

The Judge asks him of his whereabouts, but he again refuses to speak, and after some more lashes, he loses consciousness. He occasionally wakes to the sound of the Judges repeatedly questioning him, and his only response is a repetition of the phrase "the light." He again faints.

When Equality 7-2521 again wakes, he finds himself on the brick floor of a cell. He cannot move his hands but is glad that he did not betray his invention. For almost a month, the door of the cell opens twice a day, once for food and water and once for the Judges. The Judges come in order of increasing importance and ask if he will speak, but he refuses, and they leave.

The day before the meeting of the World Council of Scholars, Equality 7-2521 knows that he must escape. The Palace of Corrective Detention has old locks and no guards because men never defy the Councils and escape from the Palace. His body is healthy and strong, despite his ordeal, and he breaks down the door, sneaking outside and back to his tunnel.

Upon entering the tunnel, he lights a candle and sees that the tunnel has not been found or touched. When he sees the glass box, he ceases to care about the scars on his back. Tomorrow, he plans to take his box to the Home of the Scholars and hand them his journal as a confession. He then plans to join them in working to discover new things about his power of the sky "for the glory of mankind," and he blesses his brothers, knowing that starting tomorrow, he will rejoin society and no longer be an outcast.

Analysis:

The episode at the Palace of Corrective Detention interrupts Equality 7-2521's previous optimism, showing that despite his private experimentation with a potentially life-changing invention, the world around him has failed to change. Although the authorities know nothing about his glass box, they still identify him as a threat and punish him for his lack of obedience and his integrity. For all of their claims to serve their brothers, their questioning of Equality 7-2521 suggests that they are more interested in maintaining control than in loving all humans. The Judges are glorified torturers, although they allow the hooded men to do the physical act of beating their prisoner. The word "Judges" suggests justice and a search for the truth, but these Judges do not truly represent either.

Equality 7-2521's ordeal juxtaposes the reprehensible behavior of the collectivists with the protagonist's honor and vigor. Whereas Equality 7-2521 keeps his secret because of his conviction and need to protect his creation, the members of the Home Council show a lack of any powerful emotions. The oldest member of the Council states the command sending Equality 7-2521 to the Palace of Corrective Detention in a bored tone, suggesting the apathy engendered by collectivism. The evil authority figures in the Palace are either hidden under leather hoods or shown in a weak, bent body, and none have names or powerful descriptions. By contrast, the individualist Equality 7-2521 has a name and a distinct physical presence. His narrative emphasizes his interaction with and observation of his body, and he recovers quickly from the torture, indicating his physical and, by analogy, his mental strength.

A second contrast between Equality 7-2521 and the collectivists lies in their approach to guarding important areas. Equality 7-2521 pays a great deal of attention to the protection of his tunnel and his light, and he undergoes the Palace of Corrective Detention without revealing them. This approach is unfathomable to the authorities, who do not bother to guard their prisoners or repair their locks, a fact which also illustrates the technological regression of the collectivist era. Equality 7-2521 views the glass box as an extension of his own body, and he acts as he does because of his pride in his body, while the authorities have no sense of pride and remain careless.

The Judges have Equality 7-2521 tied to an iron post so that the men in leather aprons can whip him. The image parallels the execution of the Transgressor, or Saint of the Pyre, in an earlier section of the novel. Like the Transgressor, Equality 7-2521 is tied to a stake-like object, and he describes the iron grill of the door as "a flaming grill," while mistaking his blood for "burning coal dust." Both images bear a close connection to the flames that killed the Saint of the pyre, and both scenarios have a feeling of martyrdom. The two men willingly suffer in their bodies for the sake of an idea.

Several aspects of Equality 7-2521's imprisonment hint at the brainwashed nature of his society. The narrator escapes because no one else would have the originality necessary to even think of escape. Furthermore, although his transgression of omitting attendance at the City Theatre does not seem particularly heinous, few enough people commit any crimes that his case becomes one of paramount importance, leading eventually to questioning from "the most honored Judges of the City." Even Equality 7-2521, oddly, does not think to lie to the Judges, and he still does not wish to be a lonely outcast, retaining hope that he will be able to rejoin his community after he speaks with the World Council of Scholars. He believes that the men who he had once idolized will be greater and more enlightened than the others, but the reader may rightly remain worried that his stint at the Palace of Corrective Detention will foreshadow his reception at the World Council.

Summary and Analysis of Chapter Seven

Summary:

Equality 7-2521's next journal entry comes from the dark forest, where he waits while sleeping on the moss for the beasts. He feels old and futureless, although earlier in the morning he feels young as he carries his box to the World Council of Scholars. No one from the Palace of Corrective Detention sees him, and no one else stops him, so he enters the great hall, where he sees the blue sky through the windows and a painting of the twenty men who invented the candle. The Scholars are sitting at a long table, and they stare at the ragged intruder with surprise, but Equality 7-2521 greets them.

The oldest member of the Council, Collective 0-0009, asks for his identity, and he responds with his name and his profession. The Scholars are angry and frightened because he has broken the law, but he says that his crimes do not matter when compared to the whole of humanity. He claims that he is nothing but that he brings a gift that holds the future of mankind. He shows them the glass box and explains about his tunnel and his escape from the Palace of Corrective Detention, and they all watch his demonstration.

When the wire begins to glow red, the terrified men of the Council run to the opposite wall. Equality 7-2521 tries to reassure them, telling them that he has tamed the power and offers it to them, but they do not move. He asks them to help him use the power to benefit humanity and bring light to their cities, but their small eyes regard him with sinister intent, and Equality 7-2521 becomes afraid.

Collective 0-0009 moves to the table, leading the other scholars, and he speaks to Equality 7-2521, condemning him for breaking the law and daring to believe that a Street Sweeper could be wiser than his brothers and that he could be most useful outside of his assigned profession. Fraternity 9-3452 berates him for thinking as one person rather than with everyone else, Democracy 4-6998 sentences him to burning at the stake, and Unanimity 7-3304 wishes to lash him to death. Collective 0-0009 disagrees and says that none but the World Council has the authority to pass judgment.

Equality 7-2521 says he does not care about his own punishment but wishes to know about the fate of the light. Collective 0-0009 smiles and points out that all his brothers do not agree that he has found a new power and that if everyone does not believe it, then it is not true. International 1-5537 notes that he has worked on his invention alone and that anything not created collectively cannot be good. Solidarity 8-1164 explains that Scholars have had new ideas before but did not follow through because the other Scholars voted against them.

More members of the council speak up, with Alliance 6-7349 believing that the box is useless and Harmony 9-2642 suggesting that the box would ruin the Department of Candles, which has been approved by the multitude and cannot be destroyed by one man's work. Unanimity 2-9913 says that the box would hurt the Plans of the World Council, which are in control of the sun's rising. The World Council had recently taken fifty years to alter the Plans to accommodate the Councils for the Candle and will not do so again for some time. Similarity 5-0306 claims that the box is evil because by making life easier, it will take away from the purpose of men, which is to work for other men.

Collective 0-0009 concludes the discussion by declaring that the box must be destroyed, and the Council agrees. Furious, Equality 7-2521 calls them fools and breaks the glass of the window in order to escape. Grasping the box, he runs blindly and trips as he arrives at the edge of the Uncharted Forest. At first, he lays still, but he eventually takes the box into the forest, feeling no fear and knowing that the other men will leave him to his fate. He knows he is doomed and that he will be corrupted by solitude, but he is tired and does not care. He realizes that he built the box for himself and not for others as he had told himself, and he regrets nothing except for the fact that he will never see the Golden One again. However, he hopes that she will forget him.

Analysis:

Despite Equality 7-2521's optimism and belief that the World Council of Scholars will reward him for his invention of the glass box, his meeting with the Scholars forms the climax of the novel, after which he is irreparably cut off from his society. The Scholars' dismissal of his invention breaks his last emotional connection to the ideals of collectivism and ends the section of the story that features a conflict between man and society. After this point, the development of Equality 7-2521's understanding of ego continues, but the collectivist community is no longer a looming presence and constrictor of the protagonist's actions. The end of Chapter Seven marks the nadir of Equality 7-2521's emotions, but he enters the Uncharted Forest with no more illusions about his society.

Prior to his entry to the World Council of Scholars, Equality 7-2521 still expects that those as wise as the Scholars would be inclined to rationality over fear. Since he was young, he has identified himself in spirit with the Scholars and believes that, like him, they weigh human life and happiness over the law of the state. However, he finally learns that he has been wrong and that the entire collectivist system is flawed rather than merely some of its members. The confrontation leads him to escape from the city's confines into the Uncharted Forest, which associates nature with true knowledge and which represents his now inevitable radicalization. He ceases to justify his protection of the glass box as a benefit for humanity and accepts his true motivation as the wish to create for the sake of creation.

Rand's depiction of the Home of the Scholars contrasts the reality of the Council of Scholars with the ironic mention of "famous names" and the "illustrious men who

                                                Summary and Analysis of Chapter Seven

had invented the candle." The idea of fame suggests a certain level of separation from the common man that seems more individualist than collectivist, and accordingly the concept of invention is associated with fame and achievement. However, the candle came long before the Great Rebirth, and the members of the Council are huddled "as shapeless clouds," again emphasizing the bodiless nature of collectivism. They are confused by the presence of an intruder, for just as no one had ever thought to escape the Palace of Corrective Detention, no one has thought to interrupt the World Council, and they are particularly shocked by his low status.

The behavior of the Council of Scholars suggest that any group is ineffective and that the ills of Soviet Russia were not simply the result of faulty execution. Their insistence that all must agree in order for something to be true makes knowledge subjective, in contrast to Equality 7-2521's Objectivist ideas, and it causes stagnation as the weakest and most frightened sectors of society slow progress. They cannot agree on how to use new technology and rank obedience above prosperity or learning. Even the *de facto* spokesperson who has some mild claim to individualism, Collective 0-0009, rejects him. Significantly, the suggestions of Democracy 4-6698 and Unanimity 7-3304 equate Equality 7-2521's sin of individual thought to the only crime officially punishable by death, the speaking of the Unspeakable Word.

As Equality 7-2521 noted in the other Street Sweepers, collectivism's tenants engender fear instead of happiness as the main emotion, but while his coworkers fear the state, the Council of the Scholars are near the top of the hierarchy and fear nothing more than an active individual. They make a multitude of excuses to reject the glass box, but they recognize its efficacy and more importantly recognize the danger to their society in the possibility of rewarding Equality 7-2521. In their view, they cannot be seen to encourage free thought. At the same time, by rebuffing him, they miss a crucial opportunity to assimilate a potential radical, and Equality 7-2521 consequently sunders his remaining ties to the City.

Summary and Analysis of Chapter Eight

Summary:

Equality 7-2521 greatly enjoys his first day in the forest. He awakens from a ray of sunlight rather than from a bell, and he resists the urge to jump to his feet as he would have as a Street Sweeper. Instead, he continues to lie down and relaxes as he views the sky and the leaves.

He laughs as he realizes that he can either stay lying down or rise and do whatever he wishes. He thinks he is not making any sense, but his body rises and spins around until his hands swing him into a tree, as he celebrates his own strength. When the branch snaps, he falls back onto the moss, and he begins to roll in the moss and laugh.

He takes his glass box and goes into the forest, feeling as though he is swimming through the leaves. The trees seems to part for him in welcoming, and he joyously continues until he becomes hungry. He throws a stone and kills a bird before making a fire and cooking the bird in a delicious meal, thinking that it is so filling because he is proud of his own accomplishment.

Walking onward, he reaches a stream and, kneeling to drink, he sees his face for the first time in the reflection. He sees that his body is beautiful and trustworthy because his face is not pitiful like those of others. He continues walking until the sun sets, and he finds a hollow among some tree roots in which to sleep. Only now remembering that he is Damned, he laughs. He continues writing in his journal with paper he had hidden in his clothing, as he never gave the journal to the World Council of Scholars, but he does not understand enough of what he thinks to express it on paper.

Analysis:

After the resigned despair at the end of the previous chapter, Equality 7-2521 writes his next journal entry in an entirely different tone. His first day in the Uncharted Forest teaches him that his society's teachings about "the corruption to be found in solitude" are fabrications, and he barely thinks of his separation from the community as he explores the forest. As he journeys deeper into the wilderness, he is both physically and spiritually walking away from collectivism and the City. In *Anthem*, the only true restraint on man is other men, and the real corruption comes from the opposite of solitude. Although Equality 7-2521 does not yet have the vocabulary or the organization in his thoughts necessary to express what he has learned, his subconscious immediately recognizes and understands his new position.

The dystopian setting of the novel has certain advantages for the message Rand tries to convey. By taking collectivist ideas to their logical, if extreme conclusion, Rand offered a rebuttal to contemporary philosophers who believed that collectivism could be positive if humans did not try to take advantage of the system. Furthermore, the author chooses to explore the negative aspects of a collectivist society first so that Equality 7-2521 can recognize the full spectrum of suffering caused by collectivism before he sees the other side of the coin. The day after he leaves the City is his first experience of freedom, and he feels it more intensely because he has been deprived of it for twenty-one years. The text has thus far hinted that the end of the Unmentionable Times occurred because humanity did not appreciate what it had gained in its knowledge and principles, but Equality 7-2521 will never make the same mistake.

Despite a life in the City and no experience in the wilderness, Equality 7-2521 adopts the ways of nature with surprising facility. He has an innate connection with nature, as shown by his unconscious decision to run to the Uncharted Forest after his disastrous appearance at the World Council of Scholars. His entry into the forest purifies him, and his killing of the bird reflects his capability and his will to live, as well as his physical superiority. In Rand's narrative, he kills the bird on the first attempt, in spite of the unlikeliness of the scenario, because he is the representative man who embodies the best of human potential.

To Equality 7-2521, the needs of the body are incidental to his ability to satisfy them, and after he eats the bird, he wishes to be hungry again so that he can again feel pride in his accomplishments. His revived interest in his body recurs throughout the day. As he sees the stream of water and observes his reflection for the first time, he reverses the Greek myth of Narcissus. Whereas Narcissus saw himself and became so enamored of his image that he wasted away by the river, Equality 7-2521 sees vitality in his appearance. Rand does not describe him in detail, giving him a universal, representative quality, but he sees a beautiful, proud body just as he had previously expected. The characteristics he admires are the same that he sees in the Transgressor at the stake and the Golden One, and they in turn have recognized him for the integrity of his appearance, while the Councils also see his body and understands that they are afraid.

By entering the Uncharted Forest, Equality 7-2521 continues his transformation into the prototypical man. Unlike Adam of Genesis, however, he does not fall from the Garden of Eden by following Eve and consuming an apple from the Tree of Knowledge of Good and Evil. Instead, Equality 7-2521 is able to enter the forest precisely because he has begun to learn the truth of what is good and what is evil. His time in the Uncharted Forest cements his will to learn, although he still does not quite know what answer he seeks, and he characterizes his experience through laughter. The Council of Vocations sent International 4-8818 to the Home of the Street Sweepers because he liked to laugh, but Equality 7-2521 has regained happiness because he can laugh and sing without consequence.

Summary and Analysis of Chapter Nine

Summary:

Equality 7-2521 does not write in his journal for several days because he does not need words to record these events. On his second day in the forest, he hears footsteps behind him, so he hides in the bushes and waits. Finally, he sees a white tunic and a hint of gold, and he runs out to find the Golden One. Her hands close into fists, and her arms straighten as her body sways.

At first, she does not speak, and he does not dare approach her. In a shaky voice, he asks her why she came, and she says in a whisper that she has found him. He asks again, and she raises her head and proudly telling him that she followed him. She tells him that everyone in the City had been speaking of how he had entered the Uncharted Forest, so she ran away in the night and followed his trail into the forest.

Her tunic and arms are torn by the branches, but she does not seem to care, and she tells him that she will follow him, even if it means danger, death, and damnation. In a low but bitterly triumphant voice, she compares his eyes to fire and his proud mouth to granite and says that the other men lack hope and fire and that they are too soft and modest. Saying that she would rather be damned in his company than be blessed and remain with the others, she kneels before him.

Equality 7-2521 kneels, but instead of helping the Golden One to her feet, they kiss and embrace each other for a long time. He is startled because he has lived for twenty-one years without knowing joy. He tells her not to fear the forest or solitude and that she should forget good and evil. They decide to forget everything but their bond and their new world, and they hold hands as they continue into the forest.

They begin making love at night, and Equality 7-2521 realizes that sex is not a matter of shame but rather one of ecstasy. They walk away from the City each day, using a handmade bow and arrows to kill birds for food while gathering water and fruit in the forest. At night, they sleep in a ring of fire to protect themselves from animals. He hopes to build a house one day but is content to continue walking.

He does not understand his new, simple life, but forgets his questions as he watches the Golden One and her beauty as she walks through the forest. However, as they travel in silence, he continues to wonder about the truth of whether solitude is truly evil. He notices that although he has been taught to find joy only in working for others, he was only tired when he did so and only now finds joy as he lives for himself, and he wonders about where their thinking about morality went wrong.

One day, the Golden One tells him, "We love you," but frowns because something in the statement is not right. She then says slowly, "We are one…alone…and only…and we love you who are one…alone…and only," but they both know that they have not quite grasped something significant. They are missing an unknown word.

Analysis:

While the previous chapter concludes with Equality 7-2521 feeling that he cannot speak because he does not have the necessary understanding, he opens the next journal entry saying that he does not write because he feels recent events so intuitively that he has not needed to explain. On the one hand, he still does not know how to express his search for the Unspeakable Word. He has been increasingly articulate about his rejection of the ideals of his society, noting that he now doubts the collectivist teachings that glorify the many and castigate the individual. He knows that he has only been happy when working for himself and not for his brothers, but he cannot yet explain the error in their philosophy. On the other hand, his experience of love with the Golden One has been so logical and obvious that it has clarified the puzzle.

In his desire for truth and knowledge, Equality 7-2521 uses a rational approach much as he did with electricity, albeit with a slightly different dependent variable. When he constructed his glass box, he knew he had come closer to success when the box worked, but his search for the Unspeakable Word and for the true nature of morality is akin to the search for happiness. When he achieves happiness, as in his first day in the forest, his creation of the glass box, and his reunion with the Golden One, then he gathers another clue to the concept for which he searches. He and the Golden One continue to walk away from the City through the Uncharted Forest, and he mentions that he plans to build a house one day, although he is not in a hurry. His movement from the City to his own house parallels his search for the Word.

As Equality 7-2521 discovers love with the aid of the Golden One, he continues to equate love to the sharing of his convictions with someone of the same essence. Basing his conclusions on his trips to the Palace of Mating, he equated sex with shame, but now that it is a personal choice rather than a social fulfillment, he is no longer humiliated by the act. Love makes him happy because such a significant and now guiltless form of having a preference naturally concludes in happiness. He loves himself, and the Golden One is like himself, so their love is an extension of his self-love. However, because they do not yet have the Unspeakable Word, the Golden One is unable to tell him "I love you" with the proper implications, and they consequently feel denied.

The Golden One acts both as Equality 7-2521's lover and disciple. She continues as his foil, echoing his admirable attributes and discomfort with the teachings of their society, but she has not yet traveled as far as Equality 7-2521 has down the road away from collectivism. She feels drawn to him and chooses to break from the Home of the Peasants and follow him, but she still believes that she is damned, as evidenced by her words and her bitter, triumphant voice. She is at an earlier stage of self development, and he teaches her, informing her that solitude does not damn as the authorities have claimed.

To some extent, Rand portrays the Golden One as Equality 7-2521's disciple because she is not the main character and does not have her remaining belief in collectivism destroyed as thoroughly as his has been, but the feminist reading of her character finds her to be lacking. Rand describes her as the ultimate female, but Equality 7-2521 worships her for her appearance and her obedience only to a worthy man rather than for anything that she has actually accomplished. He gleans all her positive qualities from her body, and even his name for her, the Golden One, reflects her hair and not her real self, whereas "the Unconquered," her name for him, describes the essence of his spirit. He never follows her, and her position as the symbolic mother of humanity extends solely from his position as the symbolic father. Nevertheless, she has the aura of being his equal.

Summary and Analysis of Chapter Ten

Summary:

Equality 7-2521 begins his next journal entry sitting at a table with paper that is thousands of years old. He cannot see the Golden One sleeping on the bed in the dim light. They find the house earlier in the morning after crossing a mountain chain that has been protected by the Uncharted Forest from discovery by the Cities. Their path through the mountains is dangerous, but they know this way that no one can follow them.

At sunrise, they see what they think is a fire but actually turns out upon further investigation to be the reflection of the sun on the glass of a house's windows. The house has two stories, a flat roof, and many windows, and it is made of the same hard substance as his secret tunnel. They realize without speaking that the house must be a remnant from the Unmentionable Times, hidden by the trees from time, weather, and man.

Neither Equality 7-2521 nor the Golden One are afraid, so they enter the house of the Unmentionable Times and explore the house. The rooms are small, suggesting that only a few people lived in the house, although they find it hard to imagine that men were allowed to live in such small groups. The rooms are full of light and color, and the glass on the walls reflect instead of being transparent.

The house holds many strange objects, including globes of glass that contain metal strands such as those in Equality 7-2521's tunnel. The sleeping hall is small, with only two beds, and they are surprised that the men of the Unmentionable Times were allowed to live in groups of two. The clothes in the house are colorful, unlike the City's plain white togas and tunics, and some of the less fragile clothes still feel soft and new.

One of the rooms is full of shelves holding many manuscripts which are bound with hard leather and cloth rather than curled into rolls. They are fascinated by the small letters on the page and by some of the words which are in their language but unfamiliar, and they decide to begin reading tomorrow. After seeing all the rooms, he decides to claim the house as their own, and she agrees.

He gathers wood for the fireplace and water from the nearby stream, and he kills a goat, which he cooks in a copper pot they find in the strange cooking room. Meanwhile, the Golden One continues to stare at her reflection in the mirror. When she falls asleep on the floor after dark, he carries her to a bed and lights a candle before bringing paper from the manuscript room and sitting sleeplessly by the window.

Equality 7-2521 looks outside at the mountains and moonlight, which seem to hint at the renewal of the world. He feels that the world is waiting for his words, but he does not know what he must say. On his hands, he sees the residue of centuries which hides many secrets, and he feels both pity and respect as he ponders what his heart wishes to reveal to him.

Analysis:

The house from the Unmentionable Times connects Equality 7-2521 and the Golden One with the achievements of the past, and they feel an instinctive kinship with the house so that they feel no fear upon discovery of the building. The house is a feat of engineering, made of concrete and exhibiting the large glass windows that characterizes much modern architecture and echoes the design principles of Howard Roark in *The Fountainhead*. The light and colors throughout the house contrast the whiteness of the Home of the Students and indicate that the end of the protagonist's search for the solution to collectivism approaches, since the text often equates light with his journey toward the Unspeakable Word. He emerges from the forest and ceases to run away from the City, sensing an impending solution.

Of all the wonders in the house, the idea that only two people lived in the house surprises Equality 7-2521 the most. He originally estimates that the building must have provided the living space for no more than twelve people, a number that is astonishing to a reader from America or Western Europe, where almost everyone lives in much smaller units. In addition, his first conclusion hints at how tightly the dormitories of the City pack all of the City's citizens in the attempt to prevent anyone from ever being alone. Finally, he realizes that the house must have only provided for two people, and he is astonished and intensely curious about the Unmentionable Times.

If the discovery of the low population density of the house most astonishes Equality 7-2521, then he is most interested in the library, which he decides he will explore. He hopes that the manuscripts, which are really books, will resolve the instinctive knowledge of his body with the questions of his mind. He cannot sleep because he feels that nature is willing him to give it a sign so that he can dominate nature as man ought to do, and he suspects that the vocabulary of the books will give him the answer. He mentions that he does not recognize some of the words from the scripts, but Rand clearly indicates with his words that once he determines their meaning, he will find his own meaning.

The Golden One continues to show her physical courage as well as her submissiveness to the dominant male, as when he announces that they will live in the house, and she responds, "Your will be done." Her answer has a distinctly Biblical phrasing, again recalling comparisons to Adam and Eve and other religious or mythological first couples. Nevertheless, she displays the stereotypically female trait of vanity, choosing to stare at herself in a mirror rather than helping the narrator cook dinner. While he shares her fascination with the human body, but he chooses to act rather than merely revel in observation.

The seclusion of the house in the mountains beyond the Uncharted Forest lead to questions about how far-reaching the World Council really is. Although Rand gave the World Council a universally oppressive feel, the belief of the Scholars that the world is flat suggests that the extent of the society's influence is more limited than the authorities suggest. The limited technology of Equality 7-2521's society would also restrict the ability of the regime to maintain world-wide communication, and the mountains are not marked on the City maps, indicating that the World Council may actually control a fairly small area bordered by natural obstacles such as the Uncharted Forest. This supposition leads in turn to the question of why the society would not know about bordering civilizations. Lack of curiosity may have stifled exploration, or perhaps the wars at the end of the Unmentionable Times depopulated nearby regions. Questions of the World Council's reach do not matter greatly to a reading of *Anthem* as a parable, but they do further undermine the image of a monolithic collectivist society presented initially presented in the novel.

Summary and Analysis of Chapter Eleven

Summary:

Beginning with "I am. I think. I will" and a naming of things which belong to him, such as his hands and his spirit, Equality 7-2521 explains that he has found his answer. He stands on the mountain's peak and spreads his arms, knowing that his existence is the answer. He needs no reason to exist because he is his own reason.

He names his eyes and ears as the organs which give significance and beauty to the world. His mind and his judgment are the only things that can find truth, and his will is the only thing that can make his choices. Some words are wise and others are false, but only the words "I will it" are holy.

He knows now that he is the end of his journey, and he does not care of the overall significance of the earth because he knows about happiness. The fulfillment of happiness, in his view, is its own purpose. Furthermore, he refuses to be a tool for anyone else's accomplishments or happiness.

Declaring himself to be a man and his own miracle, he decides that he cannot share or give away his treasures of thought, will, and especially freedom. He cannot help "the poor of spirit" by giving up his own spirit. He owes nothing to his brothers, but neither does he require anything of them.

In particular, he states that he is not by default a friend or an enemy to other men because love and honor must be earned. However, he will seek friends that he respects rather than slaves or master in an unequal power relationship. They are individuals and do not need to be together except if they wish.

Continuing to speak in the first person singular, Equality 7-2521 rejects the use of the word "We" as the default word. The collectivism implicit in the word "We" does nothing but cause stagnation and the sapping away of the strength of the good, the wise, and the strong. Life is nothing if every man is subject to all others.

He declares himself as "done with this creed of corruption." He is finished with the slavery conveyed by the word "We." In its place, he substitutes the word "I," which is the god that will give men control over the earth and over their own lives.

Analysis:

Chapter Eleven begins powerfully with the simple statement "I am. I think. I will." The contrast between the softer plural pronoun "We" and these short, sharp sentences is jarring in its intensity. In reading the books in the house's library, Equality 7-2521 has rediscovered "I," the Unspeakable Word, thus fulfilling his quest and allowing him to fully articulate the philosophy towards which he has strived. With "I" newly in his vocabulary, his internal conflict and search for a replacement to collectivism have resolved, reconciling his instinct with his consciousness. His society used words to restrain him, but now he uses words to free himself from collectivist doctrine, and he recognizes that he made an error when he sought a reason for existence. His search has in one sense culminated in a word, but in the broader sense, it has culminated in his self.

His journal entry about his finding of the Unspeakable Word is not a narrative but rather the explicit statement that summarizes the goals of the novel. The tone is triumphant, as evidenced by his proud, brief sentences and the setting of the chapter on the summit of a mountain. He uses the word "I" or "my" in nearly every sentence and at the beginning of several paragraphs, as well as at the end of the entry, emphasizing the exultation that accompanies his discovery. He observes his body in the context of his surroundings, associating his mind with his body as the single entity of ego. In other novels, Rand refers to this principle as egoism, as opposed to the collectivist ideal of altruism, and she makes a secular god out of the individual's ego.

Equality 7-2521 learns to favor egoism over altruism because he has seen the evil effects of the worship of altruism. As he states in his journal, what collectivism deems righteous sacrifice is actually a thinly veiled form of manipulation and of victimization of the strong. Reflecting the views of the nineteenth-century German philosopher Nietzsche, Rand rejects the assumption that the strong and the valuable should serve the weak, and in place of this philosophy, she has her protagonist suggest that each individual should earn his own happiness and self-respect. In the society of *Anthem*, men learn to serve the state first and to place his self second, but Equality 7-2521 sees that this ideals merely take away individual rights while providing nothing in return.

The protagonist does not entirely eliminate the concept of "We," since to erase the word from the language would be the unwarranted exploitation of language through the evil omission of an entire concept, but he declares that "We" must take second place to its first-person equivalent. In other words, society cannot be a monolithic entity and must recognize itself as a group of disparate individuals. The state cannot dictate the worth of an individual, and each member of a group must see himself as a person first and a member second. Similarly, friendship and love are not obligatory groupings but the natural result of shared values, and the ability to choose one's friends make the connections stronger than they would be in a collectivist world.

By finding the inspiration for his new ideas in books from the Unmentionable Times, Equality 7-2521 returns to the individualist ideas of the Enlightenment in the Western world, as he originally did when he experimented with electricity. Although he does not say so explicitly, his main goals can be expressed as the "life, liberty, and the pursuit of happiness" of the American Declaration of Independence, which in turn reflects the writings of the Enlightenment philosopher John Locke. His ideas also apply to the economic system of capitalism, which opposed Soviet Communism

Summary and Analysis of Chapter Eleven

through much of the twentieth century. He wants each man to work at what he loves for the work's own sake, and the novel suggests society will be more productive and progressive as a result.

Summary and Analysis of Chapter Twelve

Summary:

Equality 7-2521 figures out that "I" is the word he seeks when he reads one of the books in the house. When he sees the word, he understands and weeps in pity for man, knowing why he had never felt guilt for his sins and that centuries of repression will not destroy man's spirit. He reads for days and tells the Golden One about what he learns. In answer, she looks at him and says, "I love you."

He decides that they must choose their own names that distinguish them from others as names used to do in the Unmentionable Times. He chooses Prometheus, after the ancient man who brought light from god to man and was punished for his kindness. For the Golden One, he chooses Gaea, after the earth goddess who was the mother of all other gods.

Prometheus now sees his future clearly. He recalls the Saint of the pyre, who chose Prometheus as his heir when Prometheus was only ten years old. Prometheus is now the heir of those who died for the cause of the word "I." He plans to live in his house and survive on the products of his own hands while learning more from his books.

Prometheus hopes to rebuild what the present has lost and go even further, while others with his skill continue to be held back by the weak and the dull-witted. He learns that in the past, men called his power of the sky Electricity and that electricity had been the source of many of their inventions. He decides to repair the motor that provides electricity to the house and bring light to his house. He will also use wires to create a barrier separating his property from other men because although they have the advantage of numbers, they do not have his mind.

Gaea is pregnant, and Prometheus plans to raise their son as a man who understands the concept of "I" and takes pride in his own spirit. After he learns as much as he can from his new home, he also hopes to return to the City and retrieve his friend International 4-8818, as well as those such as Fraternity 2-5503 and Solidarity 9-6347 who feel their servitude and the loss of their individuality. He plans to lead them to his home and "write the first chapter in the new history of man."

Looking on the history of men, he wonders how man had abandoned his spirit for so long when all he had to do was remain free of other men after freeing himself from gods, kings, and birthrights and declaring himself to hold inalienable rights. He gave up his freedom for the word "We" and lost everything he had made, and anyone who sought as Prometheus had to regain it was punished. He asks why men had not anticipated their fall and suggests that a few men might have foreseen it but went unheeded.

Prometheus wishes that he could tell the men who failed to stop the decay that hope still exists because "man will go on. Man, not men." He and his friends will rebuild against the decrees of other men and of the Councils, and one day he will free the cities from enslavement. To signify his fight for freedom, he will carve the immortal word "ego" into the stone of his home.

Analysis:

Following Equality 7-2521's discovery of the word "I" comes the falling action and resolution of the novel. Armed with the correct word, the Golden One is finally able to complete the sentence which had so frustrated them twice before and tell him, "I love you." Equality 7-2521 then chooses new names for both of them, taking "Prometheus" for himself because in Greek mythology, Prometheus brought fire to man and thus "taught men to be gods" and giving the Golden One the name of "Gaea," the ancient Greek name for Mother Earth. Prometheus and Gaea also have parallels to Adam and Eve in the Garden of Eden in that they plan to raise "a new kind of gods," although Prometheus' patriarchal renaming of Gaea and her humble acquiescence can be viewed as problematic.

Prometheus' ceremonial changing of names is a natural corollary to his celebration of "ego," the word that ends his narrative. By discarding their assigned names, they engage in a final rejection of collectivism and of the numerical designations that made each man a disposable part rather than a viable individual. By ridding himself of the misuse of Equality in his name, the protagonist makes a statement against the idea of compulsory equality, where equality means slavery and forcibly making everyone average rather than simply allowing to men to reach their full potential without legal restrictions. Liberty 5-3000, meanwhile, changes her name to Gaea and thus causes the idea of liberty to lose its ironic meaning. Additionally, by dispensing with the appellation "the Golden One," she shows that they do not need to describe her individual characteristics to establish her overall individuality.

After the renamings, Prometheus muses on the past and connects it to the future. He has presumably learned about the progress of the Western Enlightenment that he has unwittingly paralleled in his journal entries. He recounts the history of man as a dialectic of triumph, where man freed himself from everything that had enslaved him until the rise of socialism and other collectivist doctrines in the nineteenth and twentieth centuries, when short-sighted men willingly threw away their freedom. Rand clearly refers to the contemporary international context of the rise of Communism in the Soviet Union, which quickly turned into totalitarianism. Having completed his split from his birth society, Prometheus now sees the full dangers of collectivism and of "the worship of the word 'We,'" and he wonders how man turned away from freedom when he himself suffered so much for the cause.

Prometheus' study of the past and present causes him to decide that he will not allow the future of man to slip away in the same manner as previous history. Most of man's history has been one of progress led by the human mind, and he remains confident

Summary and Analysis of Chapter Twelve

that the human spirit will ultimately win over oppression as long as men intuitively celebrate their own minds. Like Prometheus, he plans to bring light and knowledge to his people. but he does so through the heralding of freedom in a despairing society. As he mentally reassures the men of the past who lost the battle, Rand speaks to us both in reassurance and in warning. Prometheus and Gaea will join the lessons and successes of the past to the hope of the future, and they will raise their son at the top of the symbolic and literal mountains in the knowledge that the child is a free individual.

In addition to his plans for his own family, Prometheus expects to use his force of mind and will to save others, beginning with his loyal friend International 4-8818 and the other Street Sweepers who are closest to the instinctive feeling of loss that results from their servitude. He has learned many things about science and especially electricity as a preface to his actions of liberation because he feels confident that his knowledge will protect the free and oppose the numbers of the weak and enslaved. A naturally optimistic person, he believes in the power of individualism to overcome collectivism, and he expects that his chosen friends will be worthy of his trust. After a long, introspective journey of the mind, he is ready to reengage in the conflict of the individualists against a flawed society.

Suggested Essay Questions

1. **How does the manipulation of language enforce collectivist doctrine in the society of *Anthem*?**

   One of the main motifs in the novel is the omission of the word "I" from human knowledge, as it enforces the association of the self with the group and the state in the unconscious. Over the course of the novella, Equality 7-2521 begins to recognize the need for this Unspeakable Word, but his society has not equipped him with the mental machinery necessary to work out the exact nature of what he is missing. Although he breaks away from the collective at a relatively early point, he does not understand how to offer an alternative philosophy until this block in his thinking is removed, and his search for the Unspeakable Word is a central struggle in *Anthem*.

2. **How does Rand connect Equality 7-2521's mental development to the ideals of the Enlightenment?**

   As Equality 7-2521 rediscovers electricity, he replicates the experiments of Galvani, Volta, and Franklin, all of whom lived and conducted their research during the eighteenth-century Enlightenment. Franklin was particularly involved with the founding of the United States of America and borrowed heavily from the ideas of contemporaries such as John Locke; Equality 7-2521 comes to appreciate the value of these ideals as he increasingly emphasizes an adaptation the Declaration of Independence's emphasis on "life, liberty, and the pursuit of happiness," which in turn stems from Locke's protection of "life, health, liberty, or possessions." Finally, as Prometheus, the protagonist obliquely cites Enlightenment thinkers as he discusses the history of man, who "declared to all his brothers that a man has rights which neither god nor king nor other men can take away from him."

3. **How do Equality 7-2521's experiments with electricity and the invention of the glass box influence his understanding of self?**

   Prior to discovering the tunnel and commencing his scientific experiments, Equality 7-2521 believes that the Council of Scholars is omniscient in its understanding of nature, and that he is at fault for exceeding others in a society that worships forced equality. However, after he discovers electricity, he realizes that the Council of Scholars does not know everything and that he as an individual can achieve more than any group. He also discovers that he can find happiness in experimentation because, for once, he is free to do as he wishes, and he thereby learns an appreciation for the strength of his own body. After inventing the glass box, he at first believes that he values the box because he sees its potential for humanity, but eventually, he learns that he actually loves the box because it is his creation and thus an extension of his self.

4. **Explain the connection between mind, body, and self in *Anthem*.**

At the beginning of the novella, Equality 7-2521 has a very incomplete understanding of self, so he ironically views the superiority of his mind and body as a crutch that prevents him from assimilating into his society and living morally. However, when he invents the glass box, he finally appreciates the strength of his own body and mind, and when he meets the Golden One, he learns that the connection between mind and body is particularly strong. His and the Golden One's fearless, strong bodies represent their similarly worthy minds, and, on the night of his invention of the box, Equality 7-2521 finally realizes that to take pride in one's body and accomplishments is akin to taking pride in oneself. By the end of the story, he has learned that mind, body, and self are inextricably interwoven -- and that the result is an ideal whole.

5. **In what ways does Rand reverse our usual expectations about morality in *Anthem*?**

At the heart of *Anthem* is a polemical argument that reverses our assumptions about selfishness and altruism. Collectivism operates on the expectation that if every man unselfishly works for others, all will be happier, but in Rand's extreme collectivist society, this philosophy leads inevitably to the repression of the able individual, while an egoist man will by contrast benefit society by working solely for himself. Rand also represents this apparently counter-intuitive argument through the visual association of snow white -- traditionally the hue of innocence and purity -- with the evil indoctrination of the Home of the Students, while placing Equality 7-2521's positive scientific experiments in the dark tunnel. Correspondingly, Equality 7-2521 develops the philosophy of egoism and comes to believe the opposite of what the Home of the Students taught him.

6. **What is the significance of the Uncharted Forest for Equality 7-2521?**

The Uncharted Forest serves two major functions for Equality 7-2521: it is a foreshadowing of his future, and it is an affirmation of his doubts regarding collectivism. At first, Equality 7-2521's thoughts are drawn to the Uncharted Forest because he senses that it separates the flawed collectivist society of the City from possible remnants of the Unmentionable Times with which he is obsessed. Later, his body recognizes unconsciously that the solution to his break with the World Council of Scholars lies in the forest, and he runs instinctively into it. Once he enters the Uncharted Forest, he begins a mental and physical journey away from the City, triggered by the sense of happiness and independence that he now associates with the wilderness.

7. **Explain the relationship between the Golden One and Equality 7-2521.**

The Golden One is not simply Equality 7-2521's love interest; she also serves as his first disciple, who follows him into his forest and trails the path he blazes into a rejection of collectivism. Accordingly, despite the importance of the romantic subplot in Equality 7-2521's mental development, the Golden One is a secondary character who does not exhibit the full three-dimensionality of Equality 7-2521. For him, she is a symbol, and he loves her rationally and because she instinctively shares his values and character. His love for her is also an exploration of his love for himself, which he comes to celebrate because it brings him joy.

8. **What is the significance of the house of the Unmentionable Times for Equality 7-2521?**

Sensing that his literal and metaphorical journey away from the City is coming to a close, Equality 7-2521 chooses to settle with the Golden One in the new house to create a new, individualist life where he can discover the Unspeakable Word and resolve his inner dialogue on collectivism. The house is an embodiment of the values of the Unmentionable Times, and Equality 7-2521 specifically mentions that it belonged to only two people, emphasizing its rejection of collectivist values. The house also contains a mirror in which the Golden One stares fascinated for hours, allowing her to gain Equality 7-2521's understanding of the importance of the body. Moreover, it features many electrical appliances and books which give Equality 7-2521 a fuller knowledge of what humanity has forgotten in its worship of "We."

9. **Compare the scene of the World Council of Scholars with the penultimate chapter's proclamation of "I" in terms of their respective philosophical arguments.**

The words of the World Council of Scholars encapsulate the basis and problems of collectivism, just as Equality 7-2521's words about his rediscovery of "I" constitute a manifesto in favor of egoism. Whereas Collective 0-0009 tells Equality 7-2521 that "what is not thought by all men cannot be true," Equality 7-2521 chooses to search for the Objectivist truth. He says in Chapter Eleven, "I am not a sacrifice on their altars," directly refuting the council members' claim that he must submit to the will of others and serve society as the authorities see fit. While the meeting with the Council of Scholars marks the point of no return, after which Equality 7-2521 inevitably leaves and rediscovers "I," his manifesto celebrates his discovery and allows him to justify his refusal of his society.

10. **What are some potential errors of Rand's arguments in *Anthem*?**

Because Rand chooses to argue against the most extreme possible manifestation of collectivism with the most extreme form of individualism, she does not adequately refute the supposition that a moderate form of collectivism or even a slightly altruistic society based mainly on individualism may have merit. Rand's declaration that man will most efficiently help society by focusing solely on his own works is an exaggerated version of capitalism, but in historical practice, a purely selfish approach has often led to a gap between the rich and the poor that has had more to do with lack of opportunity for the poor than with their weakness. Furthermore, Rand proposes a model based on a perfect human rationality that may only exist in theory, and one might consequently contend that Rand has made some false assumptions about human nature that rival her description of the errors of Marxism.

The Case Against Objectivism

Largely as a result of Ayn Rand's forceful, blunt personality and of her fairly extremist arguments in favor of her world view, Ayn Rand's popularity among American readers has been paralleled by an equal amount of backlash against her philosophy and against the Objectivist movement that accompanied her rise to fame. Criticisms of Objectivism have historically belonged to one of two over-arching categories. In the first category, many philosophers have either ignored or refuted Rand's arguments, contending that she has committed a number of logical fallacies in her assumptions despite her claim to perfect rationality and that she has misrepresented human nature. In the second category, others have critiqued Ayn Rand's personal application of Objectivism, as well as the cult of personality that some have alleged her Objectivist following to be.

One of Rand's major points in *Anthem* in particular is that when man lives only for others, he will cease to produce or know happiness. This assertion has some truth to it, as shown in the Soviet Union, where collectivization led directly to a decrease in per capita productivity. However, by expressing the idea that selfishness is good and the key to the running of society, Rand implies the complete denial of the power of sacrifice. Unfortunately, she chooses to argue against only the most extreme form of thankless sacrifice, effectively creating a straw man where an argument against extreme collectivism is presumed to be an argument against even moderate manifestations of societal altruism. In addition, a philosophy of ultimate self-centeredness could allow people to justify any action, so long as they feel it beneficial to themselves, and some such actions may be overly cruel or unnecessary.

Problems also occur if one analyzes Objectivism in terms of capitalism, the system most suited to egoism. Like Objectivism, capitalism rests on the assumption that society will benefit as a whole if each man is allowed to work for his own deserved reward. This assertion may be true to some extent, particularly if one believes Adam Smith's conclusion that the average worker will be protected by the "invisible hand" of the market. That being said, the history of the United States has suggested that unrestricted capitalism leads to an increasing gap between the rich and the poor caused not, as a reader of Rand might suppose, by the ability of the rich but rather by the tendency of the capable rich, in their own self-interest, to retain their wealth for their families and acquaintances, some of whom may not be as capable as they. Outside of Rand's novels, not all people have emotional attachments only to the capable, and what begins as self-interest can end in monopolies created by men who prize only money, rather than Rand's beloved inventors and creators. Consequently, anti-trust law and increased Federal regulation in the United States has altered the American understanding of capitalism, resulting in a more restricted system where self-interest is checked by law. These and other arguments do not entirely destroy the celebration of the individual proposed by Objectivism, but they do undercut its more extreme implications.

Another area in which Rand's views have often been considered objectionable is feminism. Whereas Randian heroes are often the creators and inventors of her novels, her heroines tend to fall somewhat short of equal to the men. Although women such as Dagny Taggart in *Atlas Shrugged* are capable and intelligent, they generally take a place at the male heroes' side as their lovers and disciples. Rand viewed the definition of an ideal women in terms of the ideal man; Liberty 5-3000 is an object of worship for Equality 7-2521 in *Anthem*, and she is an ideal woman largely because she submits to no one except the ideal man. However, their relationship is still inherently one of dominance, where the man is dominant and the woman submissive. Dominique Francon of *The Fountainhead* has a particularly suspect scene where her reaction to her rape by Howard Roark is one of joy as a result of her defilement. She states particularly that if Roark had treated her kindly, she would have despised him, and although Rand intends the scene to indicate that only Roark is worthy of dominating her and that only he recognizes her needs, the positive treatment of rape is nonetheless highly worrying from a feminist perspective.

Aside from the potential problems within Rand's body of work, some have suggested that Rand's treatment of Objectivism outside of her writing weakens her case. Rand seems to have deeply believed that her behavior embodied the ideals of Objectivism, and she gathered a group of disciples, which she jokingly called the Collective, who headed the Objectivist movement during the mid-twentieth century. Although her writing encouraged people to think for themselves, within the movement, her word was considered law, and disagreement tended to either be suppressed or cause schisms over the concept of ideological purity. Even her personal preferences in music were to be adopted by those within the movement, and her strong personality merely reinforced this manifestation of what some have accused to be a cult. Rand also often tended to justify her illogical desires by finding supposedly rational excuses, as when she caused the first major Objectivist schism supposedly over ideology but in reality because of her jealousy over her second-in-command's affair with another woman. Unsurprisingly, given that the Objectivists claimed to live what they preached, the facts of the Objectivist movement have also contributed to critiques of Randian philosophy.

Author of ClassicNote and Sources

Bella Wang, author of ClassicNote. Completed on July 17, 2009, copyright held by GradeSaver.

Updated and revised Damien Chazelle July 31, 2009. Copyright held by GradeSaver.

Gladstein, Mimi Reisel. The New Ayn Rand Companion. Westport, CT: Greenwood Publishing Group, 1999.

Gladstein, Mimi Reisel, and Chris Matthew Sciabarra. Feminist Interpretations of Ayn Rand. University Park, PA: The Pennsylvania State University Press, 1999.

Mayhew, Robert. Essays on Ayn Rand's Anthem. Lanham, Maryland: Lexington Books, 2005.

Sciabarra, Chris Matthew. Ayn Rand: the Russian Radical. University Park, PA: The Pennsylvania State University Press, 1995.

Ku, John. "Objections to Objectivism: A Critique of Ayn Rand's Ethics." 2009-07-17. <http://www-personal.umich.edu/~jsku/TOC.html>.

Quiz 1

1. **What name does the Golden One initially give Equality 7-2521?**
   A. the Unconquered
   B. Prometheus
   C. the Proud One
   D. the Saint of the Pyre

2. **What job does the Council of Vocations assign to Equality 7-2521?**
   A. Peasant
   B. Street Sweeper
   C. Scholar
   D. Leader

3. **How long ago was the candle supposedly invented?**
   A. 50 years ago
   B. 100 years ago
   C. 200 years ago
   D. 150 years ago

4. **What is the Unspeakable Word?**
   A. Anthem
   B. I
   C. Ego
   D. Individual

5. **What does Equality 7-2521 research while in the tunnel?**
   A. The human body
   B. Gravity
   C. Light
   D. Electricity

6. **Which Street Sweeper is too dull-witted to feel the oppression of collectivism?**
   A. Fraternity 2-5503
   B. Solidarity 9-6347
   C. Union 5-3992
   D. Alliance 6-7349

7. **Who is the head of the World Council of Scholars?**
    A. Unanimity 7-3304
    B. Collective 0-0009
    C. Union 5-3992
    D. Harmony 9-2642

8. **What does Equality 7-2521 secretly name the Transgressor?**
    A. the Unconquered
    B. the Martyr
    C. the Unburnable One
    D. the Saint of the Pyre

9. **During what activity does Equality 7-2521 escape to the tunnels?**
    A. Dinner
    B. City Hall
    C. Hymn of Equality
    D. City Theatre

10. **At what age do men join the Home of the Useless?**
    A. 40
    B. 45
    C. 50
    D. 55

11. **What is the last word in the story?**
    A. Anthem
    B. I
    C. Ego
    D. Man

12. **How does Equality 7-2521 escape the Palace of Corrective Detention?**
    A. He walks out the door uncontested.
    B. He picks the locks.
    C. He knocks out some guards.
    D. He lies to the Judges.

13. **Why does Equality 7-2521 rename himself Prometheus?**
    A. Because Prometheus brought light to man
    B. Because Prometheus invented light
    C. Because Prometheus was a king among men
    D. Because Prometheus was a Greek god

14. **What does the Golden One say to Equality 7-2521 after he discovers "I"?**
    A. I am proud.
    B. I love you.
    C. Gaea shall be my name.
    D. So it shall be.

15. **Why does Equality 7-2521 protect his glass box?**
    A. Because he is proud of his creation
    B. Because he wants to rejoin society
    C. Because he wants to sell it
    D. Because he wants to help humanity

16. **What occupation does the Golden One have?**
    A. Peasant
    B. Street Sweeper
    C. Maid
    D. Water Bearer

17. **For how long does Equality 7-2521 remain in the Palace of Corrective Detention?**
    A. 30 days
    B. 40 days
    C. 28 days
    D. 21 days

18. **Who is Equality 7-2521's first friend?**
    A. Fraternity 2-5503
    B. Solidarity 9-6347
    C. International 4-8818
    D. Democracy 4-6698

19. **Who tortures Equality 7-2521 in the Palace of Corrective Detention?**
    A. Judges
    B. Guards
    C. Punishers
    D. Council of the Home

20. **What color is the light of the glass box?**
    A. Yellow
    B. Red
    C. Blue
    D. White

21. **What crime does Equality 7-2521 not commit?**
    A. Assault
    B. Secret-keeping
    C. Obstruction of justice
    D. Theft

22. **What ended the Unmentionable Times?**
    A. Great Rebirth
    B. Great Triumph
    C. Great Fighting
    D. Great War

23. **What color are the walls of the Home of the Students?**
    A. Red
    B. Beige
    C. Black
    D. White

24. **Where does Equality 7-2521 converse with the Golden One?**
    A. On the road
    B. At the hedge
    C. On the field
    D. In the tunnel

25. **What age is the Golden One?**
    A. 16
    B. 17
    C. 18
    D. 19

Quiz 1 Answer Key

1. **(A)** the Unconquered
2. **(B)** Street Sweeper
3. **(B)** 100 years ago
4. **(B)** I
5. **(D)** Electricity
6. **(C)** Union 5-3992
7. **(B)** Collective 0-0009
8. **(D)** the Saint of the Pyre
9. **(D)** City Theatre
10. **(A)** 40
11. **(C)** Ego
12. **(A)** He walks out the door uncontested.
13. **(A)** Because Prometheus brought light to man
14. **(B)** I love you.
15. **(A)** Because he is proud of his creation
16. **(A)** Peasant
17. **(A)** 30 days
18. **(C)** International 4-8818
19. **(A)** Judges
20. **(B)** Red
21. **(A)** Assault
22. **(A)** Great Rebirth
23. **(D)** White
24. **(B)** At the hedge
25. **(B)** 17

Quiz 2

1. **Why is Equality 7-2521 pleased at the Golden One's age?**
   A. They may meet in the Palace of Mating.
   B. She has not entered the Palace of Mating.
   C. She has not yet entered the Home of the Useless.
   D. She will soon be assigned a profession.

2. **What does the Golden One offer to Equality 7-2521?**
   A. A hug
   B. A kiss
   C. Water
   D. Food from the fields

3. **Why are the Golden One and Equality 7-2521 able to talk for the second time?**
   A. Union 5-3992 has had a seizure, and everyone is preoccupied.
   B. They arrange for a secret nighttime meeting.
   C. The heat of the day is oppressive, and everyone is working far away.
   D. International 4-8818 promises not to betray his friend.

4. **What is the Transgressor's punishment?**
   A. Hanging
   B. Defenestration
   C. Beheading
   D. Burning at the stake

5. **Why is the Transgressor executed?**
   A. Refusing to perform his assigned vocation
   B. Speaking the Unspeakable Word
   C. Trying to escape the Palace of Corrective Detention
   D. Arguing against the Council of Scholars

6. **Why does the Home Council reprimand him after his meeting with the Golden One?**
   A. He arrives late to the Home of the Street Sweepers.
   B. He sings.
   C. He does not go to sleep on time.
   D. He has spoken when not permitted.

7. **How do men find partners in the Palace of Mating?**
    A. They choose among a limited list of women.
    B. Assigned by Council of the Home
    C. Assigned by Council of Eugenics
    D. Random assignation

8. **What does not characterize the Golden One?**
    A. Fearlessness
    B. Cruelty
    C. Hardness
    D. Pride

9. **What lies beyond the Uncharted Forest?**
    A. The sea
    B. A desert
    C. Mountains
    D. More Cities

10. **How many people once lived in the house of the Unmentionable Times?**
    A. 1
    B. 2
    C. 3
    D. 4

11. **What does Prometheus name the Golden One?**
    A. Europa
    B. Pandora
    C. Gaea
    D. Terra

12. **With what main emotion does the Council of Scholars view the glass box?**
    A. Disgust
    B. Suspicion
    C. Fear
    D. Fascination

13. **What excuse does the Council of Scholars not offer for the destruction of the glass box?**
   - A. The box is not accepted by the collective.
   - B. The box would wreck the Plans of the World Council.
   - C. They are afraid of the inventor's potential.
   - D. The box is useless.

14. **Where does Equality 7-2521 go after his meeting with the World Council of Scholars?**
   - A. Home of the Street Sweepers
   - B. The Uncharted Forest
   - C. His tunnel
   - D. The fields to find the Golden One

15. **Why does Equality 7-2521 think he is damned after he leaves the World Council of Scholars?**
   - A. He has lost two years' worth of work.
   - B. He has left behind his friends.
   - C. He is cast out and will be alone.
   - D. He can no longer perform experiments.

16. **Who is Equality 7-2521's father?**
   - A. Collective 0-0009
   - B. Similarity 5-0306
   - C. He does not know.
   - D. International 1-5537

17. **With whom does Equality 7-2521 discover the tunnel?**
   - A. Fraternity 9-3452
   - B. Solidarity 9-6347
   - C. Union 5-3992
   - D. International 4-8818

18. **When does Equality 7-2521 discover the tunnel?**
   - A. He finds the journal of the Transgressor and decides to investigate.
   - B. He came slightly late out of the City Theatre.
   - C. He is finding a medic for Union 5-3992.
   - D. He is sweeping the streets.

19. **Which is not among Prometheus's plans after he finishes learning everything in the library?**
   A. Attack the City
   B. Carve the word "ego" in front of his home
   C. Raise his son in freedom
   D. Gather a collection of friends

20. **How does Equality 7-2521 learn Liberty 5-3000's name?**
   A. She writes it for him.
   B. He asks her.
   C. He reads her name on her bracelet.
   D. He heard other people calling her.

21. **Why does Equality 7-2521 come near the fields of the Peasants?**
   A. He sneaks there to steal food.
   B. He brings water to the fields.
   C. He carries supplies to the Peasants.
   D. He sweeps the northern road outside of the City.

22. **At what age are women sent to the Palace of Mating?**
   A. 16
   B. 17
   C. 18
   D. 20

23. **What are Equality 7-2521's first words to the Golden One?**
   A. You are beautiful, Liberty 5-3000.
   B. What is your name?
   C. How are you?
   D. We are Equality 7-2521.

24. **How do Equality 7-2521 and the Golden One NOT indicate their affection for each other?**
   A. He calls her "our dearest one."
   B. She says that they are not siblings.
   C. She gives him a present.
   D. He says he will see her even if she is in a large group of women.

25. **Why is Equality 7-2521 sent to the Palace of Corrective Detention?**
   A. They find his glass box.
   B. He refuses to answer questions about the Golden One.
   C. He opposes the World Council of Scholars.
   D. He lost track of time in his tunnel.

Quiz 2 Answer Key

1. **(B)** She has not entered the Palace of Mating.
2. **(C)** Water
3. **(C)** The heat of the day is oppressive, and everyone is working far away.
4. **(D)** Burning at the stake
5. **(B)** Speaking the Unspeakable Word
6. **(D)** He has spoken when not permitted.
7. **(C)** Assigned by Council of Eugenics
8. **(B)** Cruelty
9. **(D)** More Cities
10. **(B)** 2
11. **(C)** Gaea
12. **(C)** Fear
13. **(C)** They are afraid of the inventor's potential.
14. **(C)** His tunnel
15. **(C)** He is cast out and will be alone.
16. **(C)** He does not know.
17. **(D)** International 4-8818
18. **(D)** He is sweeping the streets.
19. **(A)** Attack the City
20. **(D)** He heard other people calling her.
21. **(D)** He sweeps the northern road outside of the City.
22. **(C)** 18
23. **(A)** You are beautiful, Liberty 5-3000.
24. **(C)** She gives him a present.
25. **(D)** He lost track of time in his tunnel.

Quiz 3

1. **With what tone does the Home Council send Equality 7-2521 to Corrective Detention?**
    A. Boredom
    B. Sadness
    C. Coldness
    D. Anger

2. **How is Equality 7-2521 punished in the Palace of Corrective Detention?**
    A. Lashes
    B. Thirst
    C. Heat
    D. Starvation

3. **Where does I[Anthem] take place?**
    A. Europe
    B. Russia
    C. The United States
    D. Somewhere on Earth

4. **Which is not one of Equality 7-2521's experiments?**
    A. He dissects a dead frog.
    B. He works with copper and zinc.
    C. He experiments with gravity.
    D. He studies lightning rods.

5. **Why does Equality 7-2521 eventually leaves the Palace of Corrective Detention?**
    A. He finally admits the truth.
    B. The Judges threaten to execute him.
    C. The World Council of Scholars is tomorrow.
    D. He lies about his whereabouts.

6. **When does I[Anthem] take place?**
    A. In the twenty-first century
    B. In the twenty-second century
    C. Sometime in the moderately distant future
    D. In the near future

7. **What word cannot be used to describe Ayn Rand's philosophy?**
    A. Egoism
    B. Collectivism
    C. Individualism
    D. Objectivism

8. **What does one of the Street Sweepers yell in the middle of the night?**
    A. Help us!
    B. No!
    C. All wrong!
    D. Why?

9. **Why do none of the Street Sweepers talk before they go to bed?**
    A. They will be punished.
    B. They do not want to be overheard.
    C. They are too tired to talk.
    D. They are afraid to speak an unpopular opinion.

10. **Who inspires Equality 7-2521 to search for the Unspeakable Word?**
    A. The Transgressor
    B. International 4-8818
    C. The Council of the Scholars
    D. The Golden One

11. **When does Equality 7-2521 first see his reflection?**
    A. In the Uncharted Forest
    B. In a basin of water
    C. In the house of the Unmentionable Times
    D. In his tunnel

12. **When does Equality 7-2521 first wish to see his appearance?**
    A. After he meets the Golden One
    B. After he enters the Uncharted Forest
    C. After he invents the glass box
    D. After he discovers electricity

13. **What does Equality 7-2521 initially call his discovery?**
   A. The power of the fire
   B. The power of the water
   C. The power of the sky
   D. The power of the land

14. **When does Equality 7-2521 first doubt the abilities of the Council of Scholars?**
   A. After he reasons that the world is not flat
   B. After he discovers a new power in his experiments
   C. After he discovers universal gravitation
   D. After he invents the glass box

15. **What word does Equality 7-2521 decide is the trouble with his society?**
   A. We
   B. All
   C. They
   D. Every

16. **In what historical context did Rand write I[Anthem]?**
   A. The Crimean War
   B. The rise of Soviet Communism
   C. The rise of German Nazism
   D. The Cold War

17. **What point of view is used in the majority of I[Anthem]?**
   A. First-person plural
   B. Third-person limited
   C. First-person singular
   D. Third-person omniscient

18. **What form does the narration of I[Anthem] take?**
   A. Memoir
   B. Journal
   C. Letters to a son
   D. Biography

19. **Why does International 4-8818 protect Equality 7-2521?**
    A. He is afraid of Equality 7-2521's retribution.
    B. He is afraid of punishment from the authorities.
    C. He is loyal to his friend.
    D. He rejects the tenets of their society.

20. **Why does the Golden One enter the Uncharted Forest?**
    A. She is escaping punishment.
    B. She wishes to explore nature.
    C. She wants to give Equality 7-2521 a parting gift.
    D. She wishes to follow Equality 7-2521.

21. **Why does Equality 7-2521 want to see his reflection?**
    A. Idle curiosity
    B. To feed his self-esteem
    C. To take pride in his body
    D. To know if he is worthy of the Golden One

22. **What is the only capital punishment crime in this society?**
    A. Speaking against the society's principles
    B. Committing murder
    C. Refusing an assignment from the Council of Vocations
    D. Using the Unspeakable Word

23. **Which is not juxtaposed in I[Anthem]?**
    A. The individual and the collective
    B. Happiness and fear
    C. Rationality and irrationality
    D. Anarchism and government

24. **What punishment does the Council of Scholars NOT suggest for Equality 7-2521?**
    A. Lashing to death
    B. Crucifixion
    C. Turning over to the World Council
    D. Burning at the stake

25. **Why is the Council of Scholars initially offended by Equality 7-2521's presence?**
    A. He has revolutionary ideas.
    B. He is a Street Sweeper.
    C. He is a prisoner.
    D. He has interrupted an important vote.

Quiz 3 Answer Key

1. **(A)** Boredom
2. **(A)** Lashes
3. **(D)** Somewhere on Earth
4. **(C)** He experiments with gravity.
5. **(C)** The World Council of Scholars is tomorrow.
6. **(C)** Sometime in the moderately distant future
7. **(B)** Collectivism
8. **(A)** Help us!
9. **(D)** They are afraid to speak an unpopular opinion.
10. **(A)** The Transgressor
11. **(A)** In the Uncharted Forest
12. **(C)** After he invents the glass box
13. **(C)** The power of the sky
14. **(B)** After he discovers a new power in his experiments
15. **(A)** We
16. **(B)** The rise of Soviet Communism
17. **(A)** First-person plural
18. **(B)** Journal
19. **(C)** He is loyal to his friend.
20. **(D)** She wishes to follow Equality 7-2521.
21. **(C)** To take pride in his body
22. **(D)** Using the Unspeakable Word
23. **(D)** Anarchism and government
24. **(B)** Crucifixion
25. **(B)** He is a Street Sweeper.

Quiz 4

1. **Why does the Council of Vocations give Equality 7-2521 his job?**
   A. Because he is too independent to be allowed a higher position
   B. Because they have no other positions
   C. Because they think he needs to learn the value of work
   D. Because they regard him as a worthy individual

2. **What does Equality 7-2521 realize is the true meaning of things?**
   A. His service is.
   B. He is.
   C. His creativity is.
   D. Humanity is.

3. **How does Equality 7-2521 define friendship?**
   A. As a natural condition of man
   B. As a phenomenon that defies all logic
   C. As the product of choice
   D. As his feeling for all men

4. **What does Equality 7-2521 feel is the trouble with his society?**
   A. It tells him that he cannot be happy.
   B. It has brutal purges of its members.
   C. It teaches him that he cannot be honest.
   D. It teaches that he owes others because of his ability.

5. **Where does Equality 7-2521 write as he exults in his discovery of the Unspeakable Word?**
   A. In the library
   B. In the branches of a tree
   C. At the summit of a mountain
   D. At his window

6. **What is NOT notable about the house of the Unmentionable Times?**
   A. The paintings
   B. The architecture
   C. The mirrors
   D. The number of inhabitants

7. **Why does Equality 7-2521 name Liberty 5-3000 the Golden One?**
    A. Her hair
    B. Her skin
    C. Her smile
    D. Her clothes

8. **To what does Equality 7-2521 compare the Golden One?**
    A. A blade of iron
    B. A storm
    C. A flower
    D. A sunrise

9. **When is Equality 7-2521 allowed to speak to non-Street Sweepers?**
    A. While on break
    B. During dinner
    C. At the Social Meetings
    D. At the City Theatre

10. **Where does Equality 7-2521 spend his first five years?**
    A. Home of the Nurseries
    B. Home of the Caregivers
    C. Home of the Infants
    D. Home of the Mothers

11. **Where does Equality 7-2521 spend his late childhood and adolescence?**
    A. Home of the Disciples
    B. Home of the Apprentices
    C. Home of the Children
    D. Home of the Students

12. **Why was Equality 7-2521 unhappy when young?**
    A. He was too tall.
    B. His classmates disliked him.
    C. His classes were too easy.
    D. He had chronic depression.

13. **Who does Equality 7-2521 try to imitate when he is studying?**
    A. Fraternity 2-5503
    B. Solidarity 9-6347
    C. Union 5-3992
    D. International 4-8818

14. **What is Equality 7-2521's initial response to his assignment by the Council of Vocations?**
    A. Annoyed
    B. Proud and happy
    C. Relieved
    D. Upset

15. **What subject does Equality 7-2521 particularly love?**
    A. Science
    B. History
    C. Math
    D. Literature

16. **How is Equality 7-2521 NOT different from his peers as a child?**
    A. He commits the crime of preference.
    B. He is too interested in girls.
    C. He fights with the others.
    D. He asks too many questions.

17. **What are the City Theatre plays about?**
    A. How good toil is
    B. The battle of the sexes
    C. The advantages of their society
    D. The glory of their leaders

18. **What does Equality 7-2521 call his "second Transgression of Preference"?**
    A. His desire to exceed others
    B. His desire to become a Scholar
    C. His dislike of Union 5-3992
    D. His attraction to the Golden One

19. **How do Equality 7-2521 and the Golden One initially greet each other?**
    A. With subtle gestures
    B. With waves
    C. With yells
    D. With salutes

20. **What does Equality 7-2521 believe will be his fate in the Uncharted Forest?**
    A. Thirst
    B. Death from a beast
    C. Weariness
    D. Starvation

21. **Who were the Evil Ones of the Unmentionable Times?**
    A. The murderers
    B. Probably our society
    C. Those who corrupted children
    D. The ones across the ocean

22. **What expression was on the dying Transgressor's face?**
    A. A smile
    B. Sadness
    C. Anger
    D. A twisting of agony

23. **How does Equality 7-2521 construct the glass box?**
    A. With the help of a rogue Scholar
    B. With materials from the tunnel
    C. With materials he stole from the Home of the Scholars
    D. With items from the Home of the Street Sweepers

24. **What does Equality 7-2521 say after he makes the glass box?**
    A. This is our creation.
    B. We made it. We created it.
    C. It is done.
    D. I am the maker.

25. **To what does Equality 7-2521 compare the Council of Scholars?**
   A. Waiting hawks
   B. Slimy eels
   C. Crouching tigers
   D. Shapeless clouds

Quiz 4 Answer Key

1. (**A**) Because he is too independent to be allowed a higher position
2. (**B**) He is.
3. (**C**) As the product of choice
4. (**D**) It teaches that he owes others because of his ability.
5. (**C**) At the summit of a mountain
6. (**A**) The paintings
7. (**A**) Her hair
8. (**A**) A blade of iron
9. (**C**) At the Social Meetings
10. (**C**) Home of the Infants
11. (**D**) Home of the Students
12. (**C**) His classes were too easy.
13. (**C**) Union 5-3992
14. (**B**) Proud and happy
15. (**A**) Science
16. (**B**) He is too interested in girls.
17. (**A**) How good toil is
18. (**D**) His attraction to the Golden One
19. (**A**) With subtle gestures
20. (**B**) Death from a beast
21. (**B**) Probably our society
22. (**A**) A smile
23. (**B**) With materials from the tunnel
24. (**B**) We made it. We created it.
25. (**D**) Shapeless clouds

Made in the USA
Middletown, DE
22 March 2018